27 + 27

One Woman, One Life, One Truth

Edwin Paul Franklin

WESTBOW
PRESS
A DIVISION OF THOMAS NELSON
& ZONDERVAN

WestBow Press books may be ordered through booksellers or by contacting:

WestBow Press
A Division of Thomas Nelson & Zondervan
1663 Liberty Drive
Bloomington, IN 47403
www.westbowpress.com
1 (866) 928-1240

Because of the dynamic nature of the Internet, any web addresses or
links contained in this book may have changed since publication and
may no longer be valid. The views expressed in this work are solely those
of the author and do not necessarily reflect the views of the publisher,
and the publisher hereby disclaims any responsibility for them.

Any people depicted in stock imagery provided by Thinkstock are
models, and such images are being used for illustrative purposes only.
Certain stock imagery © Thinkstock.

ISBN: 978-1-4908-3560-0 (sc)

Library of Congress Control Number: 2014907661

Printed in the United States of America.

WestBow Press rev. date: 04/23/2014

FOREWORD/ REVIEWS

Victor Jacob, Laboratory Technologist, Abu Dhabi

This book will have you captivated from cover to cover. It's an inspiring story which explains the bigger and better plan for our life. How this one woman's life as a daughter, wife, mother, mother-in-law and grandmother is lived out purposefully is truly amazing. This is a story of finding the truth and love that strengthened her internally to endure life's hardships and fight through them with great endurance.

Deborah, USA

I was truly intrigued by this story. It is very heartfelt and reveals a lot about how different lives around the world impact each of us, no matter our race, religion, gender or class. This woman's story is profound, and that she proved that no matter what our "lot" in life, it all still serves as purpose to and for our Creator. I would love to see this book reaching many readers around the world.

Mary Princess Lavanya, Professor, Loyola College, India

I congratulate the author on the narrative style adopted by him to keep the readers with the same interest till the end, which very few authors' can do. I salute brave Amsaveni who lived by faith and endured everything. The love and the bond between Amsaveni and Edwin cannot be worded and every reader will be blessed and begin to be a blessing on reading it. I am sure that this book will bring many to the light with the unquenchable thirst to find what happened next and how. This book will be a key for revival in the 21st century.

Aneeja Mariam Joseph, Head of Training, Pallium India
*This book is the heart speaking, intriguing, genuine and inspiring. So
was Amsaveni in real life. Her character and faith is truly commendable.
She turned every hurdle into a stepping stone; every time she fell, she
rose with greater strength and grace, pulling others too to their feet and
inspiring them to run the life's race. I was blessed by her and I am sure
many will be blessed by this book.*

Prof. D. Prince Annadurai, Madras Christian College, India
*I appreciate the author in bringing out this wonderful and remarkable
work in remembrance of Mrs. Amsaveni. Though I have not met her
directly, a few telephone conversations with her were unforgettable.
She was a woman with courage, faith, highly motivated and cheerful
despite all odds. She was a living example of a wise woman and was
always filled with compassion, praise and worship. It will not be just
enough to say that she was a prayerful person, but the entire life of her
was dedicated for praying for others. Though the path she travelled in
her personal life was thorny and arduous she always has been spreading
a positive vibe and strength to the people around her.*

*Last time when this author visited his alma mater, he initiated
a scholarship on Amsaveni's name (**Amsaveni Gold Medal Award**)
which will be given to a poor and needy I MSW student every year.
His unquenching love for Amsaveni is inspirational to many youngsters
especially in the fast raced materialistic world of today. A book on
his inspired woman will be an epitome of her prayerful life and her
encouragement to the lives of many around her.*

Shekinah Devarakonda, Business Analyst, USA
*The life's additions, subtractions, multiplications and divisions invited
her to a Well to swallow her sorrows promising false rest and peace.
But He became the Living water; quenched her thirst by granting the
real peace both in life and eternity!!! 27+27, a book with right equations
for our life.*

Christopher Darla, Evangelical Community Church, Abu Dhabi
Though we believe that great events such as death or a birth are guided by the hand of the Creator, yet we drift into a feeling that our daily lives are the product of our own efforts. This book brims with penetrating stories and insights that show us otherwise. This book examines our backgrounds, our disappointments, our triumphs, our beliefs and explains how they are all part of the intentional and perfect work of our Master Creator!

Rosetta D'Souza –Jerrin, Abu Dhabi
Some people live lives that are so extraordinary and supernaturally orchestrated that it can any day shame the famed fables and myths; Amsaveni was definitely one of them! She was lifted out of the ashes of shame, brokenness and even death to a genuinely blessed and complete life, a feat that can neither be explained nor accomplished by man alone. I am privileged to read this amazing journey where death collides with faith and births into a legacy! And who else is better equipped to explain this legacy apart from the author who knew her very closely? I see Amsaveni standing boldly before her Creator with tearful eyes of joy, quivering lips of prayers and a peaceful heart of love. The true events revolving around a family and especially the life of Amsaveni tucked away in a remote corner of South India is not just a feel good story of overcoming trials but an infallible evidence of a power beyond the barriers created by human society and human wisdom.

Vason Jabbok, Assistant Commandant,
Central Reserve Police Force, India
The author has crafted a beautiful story based on the life of a woman who was once full of despair but then found hope. 27+27 exposes the reader to a woman's journey of struggling through a meaningless life of self-imprisonment to the life which was full of purpose, peace and success. You may be asking yourself how this marvelous transformation occurred and who the Transformer was. It is here, in the pages of this book, that you will find your answer. If you are searching for your life's purpose this book has the answer. I invite you for an exciting journey from darkness to marvelous light; from mundane living to eternal glory.

Vithya J, IT professional, India

We meet a lot of people who inspire us instantly. Is she one of them? No. She is someone who would make you inspired for the rest of your life. As I read this book, I thought, how many times in life have we felt 'that's it, Now, I don't want to live anymore', 'am giving up, it's enough'. Do we all really have a strong reason to give up every time and ask for death? Well, we know the answer. But she did have a reason to give up, yet she chose to live. She lived her life in complete and had made a significant impact in many people's lives. This book made me think "Why not live- life to the fullest?" Thanks to the author.

Wildon Calvin Fernandes, Quality specialist, Abu Dhabi

As the title of the book kept surprising me and made me curious to find about"27 + 27", i was thrilled to find a perfect equation. An equation of the former years of dejection, despair, anguish is compensated with acceptance, joy, peace in later years .I welcome, applaud & commend this excellent book which this author brings out to bless us. The readers as they read about this One Woman's extraordinary life changing story, surely will experience the equation in their life as they read through the pages to know that it's their loving father, the Maker , the Creator who is waiting eagerly to bring that Joy, Peace and hope to them unconditionally.

Dr. Ramesh R, Oncosurgeon, India

This book strongly inspires and challenges all those who give-up so easily their efforts, mental strength and even their life too for mere stress and failures in our daily life. I was privileged to witness very closely a part of Amsaveni life in the recent years and had wondered the faith and prayer she exercised had definitely overpowered any medical advancement. Really this book is a masterpiece, witnessing the grace of Almighty in turning the impossibilities of a human life into an exemplary life. This book is also a love display of the depth to which Almighty can shower His blessings over one true human who believes Him from the depth of her heart. Her life story is a true help to this generation beyond age, sex, race and religious disparities.

Dr Joseph Xavier Latha, Head of Welfare, Abu Dhabi

Mother's love is so special, a never-ending gift. The woman mentioned in this book is known to me, she had made her total life profitable and prayerful not only for her family but to all the relationship she gained out of love. She was the one who brought new insights, stimulation to the relationship and a new dimension in finding and tasting 'THE LOVE OF GOD'. I have not seen her personally but her tender voice lingers holding a special place in my hearts and stir my emotions whenever her name is remembered. This book will be really appreciated by every woman, especially the mothers.

Melwyn John Neelankavil, Canada

How often does one be fortunate enough in life to be a witness to a life changing experience? An experience that changes the very way you think and act, that convinces you that you are not here by accident and that you are here for a purpose. The characters in this book have gone through what I like to call "the two extremes in life" - the lowest form of depression and the kind of happiness that one can only dream of. I invite you to be a part of this wonderful experience and be assured of the fact that in the midst of our trials, our Lord, Jesus Christ will always be by our side, encouraging us to keep pressing on towards His Kingdom, and when our mission is complete, to reign with Him forever.

Raymond Joseph, Pastor, Church for All Nations, Abu Dhabi

This book talks about the journey of Amsaveni's life and her courage, determination and dependency on her Creator. Her life experiences, those that are unfolded in this book, not only inspires us but challenge and encourage us to trust the love of our Heavenly Father in the midst of adverse situations and sufferings.

Angelene Suriya Benjamin, Head of Institutions, India

It is my hope that others may enjoy these varied glimpses of this book and that the Lord whom she loved and served may be glorified. Mrs. Amsaveni conveyed to this young author and hungry Christians the essential ingredient of the new nature – a Christlikeness which was appealing. A book like this owes much too many. I warmly commend this book.

.

DEDICATION

To my inspiring mother
&
To my two delights ("Fiammetta" & "Danita")

CONTENTS

DECLARATION

The lives mentioned in this book are not fictitious. All the situations and experiences mentioned in this book are real and have taken place. The Author is the witness for most of the expressed content. Any clarification required in the content of the book can be sought from the author directly without any hesitation.

ACKNOWLEDGEMENTS

I'm humbled by the overwhelming response and genuine support from each of my friends who had encouraged me, stood with me and facilitated me to get my first book into publication.

With reverence I acknowledge my Savior's everlasting grace and favor in enabling me to initiate the thought, to complete the writing and to publish this book within a year.

In specific my sincere thanks go to Melwyn John Neelankavil from Canada and Rosetta D'Souza Jerrin from UAE for their timely support in all my critical times during the writing of this book and to each one of those who wrote the foreword and testimonials for this book.

Finally, my beloved wife Roshni Franklin for her understanding and love and to my father who helped in arranging the facts and provided clarity as and when needed.

PREFACE TO THIS BOOK

"Success is never instantaneous. It evolves from
a journey with time, people and purpose"
-Edwin Paul Franklin

None of us, who are reading this right now, were given these three important choices when we were born. (1) To choose our parents, (2) To choose our physical appearance or intellectual ability and, (3) To choose our place of birth or country. If that was possible, then we may have been better prepared to be where we want to be, to be in the family which we desire and to be in the country where we feel comfortable, safe and secure. But for instance, if these choices were given to us before we are formed in our mother's womb, the irony is that we would not have any idea or clue on whom to choose and what to choose either.

On the other hand, if our parents are given that choice to form their child in the womb, the color of skin, the intelligence level for their child, the depth of discipline, the quality of character, the much desired success etc., then no parent would have any troublesome kids or in some cases, any mentally challenged kids.

The birth of a child is not an accident. Moreover, it's not just the physical relationship of a man and woman that brings forth the creation of a child in the womb. If that was the case, there wouldn't be any barren women at all. The 36-40 weeks of a fetus forming in its mother's womb is not only natural, but also a mystery. From a race of millions of life cells (sperms) to reach its egg, and thereby forming a zygote or fertilized egg and staying there for approximately 250-280 days, (6000-6720 hours, 3,60,000 – 4,03,200 minutes), guarded and protected amidst the dark chambers of the womb surrounded by blood, tissues and fluids inside another living body is definitely a mystery. The brain, the cells, the tissues, the eyes, the face, and every single part of the body are fearfully and wonderfully made. Then on the appointed day, what we call as 'Birthday', the fetus formed in the womb enters a new world – our planet Earth.

So, birth in itself is a planned journey for a period of time, from that moment the fetus is formed in the womb, and grown for another period of time and delivered as a baby to this world. THE IMPACT of this one fetus and its growth, its life time's ups and downs, its achievements, its trials, its temptations, the financial, physical and emotional changes, and its quest for a fulfilling life, etc. is not less than beyond our imagination. Finally, the embryo's life ends with the title of a 'corpse' or a 'dead body' or a 'set of remains'. This is indicated by the halted blood circulation or cell growth or heart beat; the moment at which life ends, is also a dreadful mystery.

Just as the fetus entered alone into this world, it also departs alone from the world. Throughout this journey of approximately 9 months, the fetus which is formed in the womb delivered as a baby and from there on lived on this earth; its tenure definitely leaves behind an impact, and goes back to its Creator.

"It is HE that hath made us and not we ourselves"

Any creation exists today because of the Creator who existed from infinity. There can be no creation without a Creator. Any creation can only be an outcome of the thought, ideas and strength of its Creator. In simple words, A Creator is the Supreme Being who creates and sustains the creation. He is the source of all life and breath, the maker of the sun and moon that we see every day and the Keeper of all living things.

The purpose of this book is simple yet profound. This book deals with one such creation of the creator, "The Woman". The woman is the most important part of the creation and the first cradle for any human who is subjected to many physical and emotional challenges, and yet endures a divine purpose. The woman's life which is mentioned in this book is brought to the attention of the reader, in order to see her life story the way I personally witnessed and wondered. The life she lived between deadly situations, the endurance of her life amidst countless struggles, the perseverance with which she handled herself and her responsibilities, and the one true secret by which she overcame death's stings and lived a victorious life right. This book was written within a year after she departed this world and is in a better place. (Yes, February 5, 2014 is her first death Anniversary).

Everyone has problems. No one ever can deny this. Every problem leaves us with an experience. Every experience creates an IMPACT. Does every IMPACT from our life's experiences elevate us to excellence? This book deals with the three main characters of a middle class family from South India. Every chapter deals with a set of facts and thrilling moments the three protagonists pass through in their daily lives, the profound effect that was created from their life's experience in every timeline at different stages of their lives. All of them have faced unimaginable adversities from all aspects of life, each in their own measure.

Interestingly, each main protagonist at their predestined point in life had moved towards a unique experience. From then on and further, each experience they encountered had only led them to excellence. The life's situations remained the same, the people remained the same, and the hardships remained the same, but at times the environmental surroundings worsened than before. But the IMPACT they experienced within, had changed their perception, attitude and thinking towards life. This was the one unique experience they had surpassed their logical thinking and cognitive understanding and thus outshined each of them. This book will explain one of the characters in depth, "Amsaveni".

"The two most important days in your life are the day you are born and the day you find out why"
- Mark Twain

This book is mainly written for you. I personally believe that each chapter will give the added edge, an impact that challenges every experience of your life to move towards your life's unique purpose. Not every experience we face excels us.

But the one unique experience which is explained in this book, which Amsaveni had experienced, at some point of your life, I pray you will also experience that will surely elevate the whole perception, goal and objective of your current life to a much greater extent than you can perceive.

With that hope, every page is written thinking of you. I hope that this book will be a help which you'll take at least one percept of each chapter to apply wherever suitable in your daily life.

"Winning does not start around you, it begins inside you"
— Mike Murdock

Enjoy reading!
Yours sincerely

Author

CHAPTER 1

A man named ALWARAPPAN

1956 till 1980:

Thoothukudi also known as Tuticorin, (the name stands for its magnificent natural resources and amazing people it had produced in the past and even today), is a district in the state of Tamil Nadu in Southern India. The district is known for its pearl cultivation, with an abundance of pearls being found in the seas offshore. It is known as the gateway of Tamil Nadu and it has one of the major seaports in India with its history dating back to the 6th century A.D. The Thoothukudi district has given India many great freedom fighters, like V. O. Chidambaram Pillai, Oomaithurai, Veerapandiya Kattabomman and the great poet Subramanya Bharathi, etc. It is from this port V O Chidambaram Pillai sailed on the first Indian Swadesi Steamer S. S. Gaelia on 1 June 1907. The people here are part of a unique culture of food, tradition and lifestyle.

Sathankulam is a small town in Thoothukudi district. This town is well known for its economic solidarity, and is heavily involved in cultivation of paddy, groundnuts and jaggery. Several people have shifted their trade to education, retail trade and office jobs. Thus the economy of the people is based on various sources. In this town lived the late Mr. Murugesan Pillai, with his spouse, the late Mrs. Kalyani Krishnaveni. A very courteous and heartwarming family, they had a rich cultural background and belonged to the

Tirunelveli Saiva Pillai community (a landowning upper caste, feudal community), which is a subcaste or branch of 'Saiva Pillai'. They have been the original Landlords and their major source of income would come from agriculture. Their family also exhibited love for the society, and was considered to be one of the respected families in that town.

The family is also known for its spiritual standards where every morning the men in the family would come after bathing with a wet towel wrapped around their waist and conduct pooja in front of the prayer room in their house. The ladies in the house would fast for various deities time and again as a custom.

Mr. Murugesan Pillai worked under the Clerical Department in the Royal Indian Air Force at Kangenchunga, Davalagiri hill stations at Allahabad a district in North India from 1942 to 1947 until Indian Independence. Obliging the family values and love towards his ailing father, he refused an offer that paved him a job at London (as his superior was well pleased with his competencies and would like to take him along) soon after independence. Since, he wanted to take care of his father and his family; he came back from the Allahabad to his home town. The then Government had provided him the privilege and official permission to sell Postal Stamps and Government bonds, which contributed to the additional income for his family.

Apart from this, his family had 50-75 acres of fertile land, which yields bags of rice every monsoon for the needs of the family and remaining household. Also, the family owned 5-6 houses which were given for rent thereby adding to the monthly income to the family. Being friendly, he was called as "Vendor Pillai", as he was the only one authorised to sell the Government bonds in that town, and gained respect and honor among his community members. He was blessed with seven children, six sons and one beloved daughter. The family was well known in the society and had lived a modest life.

Among out the six sons he had, our first protagonist is the third born son ALWARAPPAN born on a Wednesday, 11th January 1956. He was named after his Grandfather, whom his father loved and respected a lot. In the context of South Indian culture, naming after one's grandfather amidst other grand children in the family is a symbol of privilege and prestige given to that grandson by the parent. Also the name of the head of the house will not be uttered by the wife or any woman of the house, except the Mother or the Father thereby carrying a ton of respect and honour. Even so, his name also signified one of the respected Tamil poet-saint of south India who lived between the 6th and 9th centuries AD (and espoused 'emotional devotion' or bhakti in their songs of longing, ecstasy and service). He was named thereby to express their support and love towards their Tamil language and culture.

He and his two elder brothers were the only privileged to do their higher studies after their schooling. The eldest brother went to be trained as a teacher, a job - guaranteed course in those days. Soon enough, after his training, he was offered a job as a high school teacher and then he moved from his hometown to another place and thereon settled down for his lifetime. The second eldest brother after his schooling was enrolled in Tiruchirappalli, Regional

Engineering College, one of the renowned old colleges of Tamil Nadu. The third son, Alwarappan after his high school wanted to become a Tamil Literature Pundit, as his love towards Tamil was abounding. But his father wouldn't permit his son to follow his dreams instead, he wanted him to pursue Economics and move on with his career. Against his wish, his father enrolled him in the V.O. Chidambaram Pillai College, Thoothukudi for him to pursue Economics. His younger brothers and only sister were still pursuing their schooling till this time.

Having been born with a silver spoon in his mouth, growing up in a wealthy atmosphere, Alwarappan dealt with life very casually. He used to go to college just for the sake of going, as his father compelled him to study subjects he didn't like. Strangely, he didn't mingle with his peers. His favourite spot in the college was the college canteen, where he could spend his money to buy ice cream and eat. His father and mother had pampered him so much and always provided him all what he wanted. Every time he came home, he prefer to eat roasted groundnuts and his mother would still make a large quantity of it before his arrival and feed him to his heart's pleasure. He had been in the comfort zone all through his teenage years.

He was never in a situation to face the tough side of life, or had need to focus seriously on education or on getting a job. He was only interested in eating, reading books in the library, writing poetry and sleeping. He was very short-tempered and was always lazy to do any work. As he was always in the comfort zone, life didn't mean serious to him either. On the spiritual side, he used to participate and sing religious bajan in the month of the Tamil year (Margali). He was so proud of the fact that at the young age of fourteen he was a devotee to the religion. Having negative thoughts against other religions, he started preaching against them. He also started printing leaflets on his religions' slogans and distributing them. Also he studied the famous Thirukkural (a classic of couplets or Kurals (1330 rhyming Tamil couplets) or aphorisms. It was authored by Thiruvalluvar, a poet who is said to have lived anytime between 2nd century BC and 5th century AD.

Most believe he wrote Thirukkural in 30 BC which is part of Tamil Sangam Period. It is one of the Tamil books of Law). He was also proud about his family wealth and property due to which he thought highly of himself and thus looked down at his peers in school and college days.

Meanwhile, the family was slowly going through a financial crisis. The income from the vending stamps/bonds business, the land and the house rent was not sufficient to meet all the needs of the 7 growing children. The relatives never happy with the growth and wealth of the family were waiting for the day of their decline. From the eldest son, even though, each one got into a professional course and started settling down, their income was never enough to sustain their own families and hence they were not in a position to provide any financial support to the family back home.

Before they realised, the whole family ended up bankrupt and was put in a situation to sell their properties in order to survive. The sons who were grown up and educated didn't come forward to take up the mellowing family's economic status.

Each one in their own capacity was trying to make their own ends meet. But the time had come when they were losing one property after another and the society witnessed their gradual decline and saw them ended up with nothing, not even food for the next day.

At this point, the family migrated to a different district in Tamil Nadu, "Salem" and settled in "Shevapet", a busy place in Salem.

CHAPTER 2

A woman named AMSAVENI

1959 till 1980:

Salem is a city and a Municipal Corporation in Salem district in Tamil Nadu. It is also known as the "Mango City". Malgova from Salem is very sweet. Also, the Salem Steel Plant exports stainless steel to other countries. It is the fifth largest city in Tamil Nadu in terms of population, and is very powerful both economically and politically and it's a part of Western Tamil Nadu and is located at the base of the popular tourist destination near to Yercaud hills. Salem is one of the major producers of traditional silver anklets, which are sought after by most women. It boasts of large textile, steel, automotive, poultry and sago industries. It also has one of the largest magnesite deposits in India and also has rich bauxite and mineral reserves. Silk and cotton fabrics from Salem are sold throughout Tamil Nadu and are a big buy.

The Indian Institute of Handloom Technology, the second of its kind in India is found here. The uniqueness of this city's name is that every letter stands for the rich resources it contained in its geographical space, S- for Steel, A–for Aluminium, L–for Limestone, E- for Electricity and M– for Mango.

The Shevapet is a host business spot of Salem City. It is also a well-known market place and an important economic zone of the city. Here in one of the schools worked the late Mr. Sundaram Pillai, a strict school teacher who was well known for his white dhoti and modest character. After he lost his parents at a very young age, he and his sister grew up in their uncle's home. His uncle cheated him on all his property which he had inherited from his parents. Yet, he was very studious and disciplined, since his father was a lawyer and had taught him strict work principles. After his studies, he completed training in teaching, got hired and started teaching in a Government school. He married the late Mrs. Pattammal, the second daughter of a well-known teacher from that area. He gave his daughter Pattammalin marriage after knowing the honest and hardworking nature of Sundaram Pillai. Pattammal, used to take financial support from her father quite often as her husband Sundaram Pillai's income was not enough to cater the needs of her six daughters and one beloved son. (This is an interesting contrast to Alwarappan's family of six sons and one beloved daughter).

Though Sundaram Pillai used to work in a Government position, the income was menial and hence he took tuition in Maths and Science at home to bring in additional income.

Nevertheless, the family had more needs than wants. Following tradition, the daughters of the family were not sent for higher studies after schooling. They had to be married off as soon as possible. However the son was given more importance. He was sent to the Government Arts College

Salem, one of the best known Colleges in the city to pursue his graduate degree in Mathematics.

The eldest daughter, one the smartest in the family was excelling in her studies and was very supportive towards the family in helping her mother in all household works and her father during the tuition classes. She was very affectionate to her immediate brother, the only son of the family. She was like the next mother for him, in disciplining him, explaining him the family's situation and preparing him mentally to support the family as soon as he can. Also she had inculcated a sense of fatherly responsibility to take care of all her five 5 sisters.

Alas! One day she got a severe stomach ache, and was battling through the pain at her school. She was immediately rushed to the hospital, but the hospitals were not equipped to deal with this sickness in those days. Sadly, in a day's time she passed away at her teenage which was a huge blow to the family.

The second eldest daughter (Thanam – name changed) was not keen on studies but desired to explore the world at any given opportunity. Soon, she was married to one of the close relatives in a temple in a very simple manner, and she migrated to Chennai as her husband worked there.

The third daughter of the family was born on Monday, December 28, 1959, and was considered to be the lucky charm of the family. Soon after her birth, the family acquired property from Pattammal's father and she was considered as a blessing to her family. She was named AMSAVENI, meaning all blessings and prosperity perfectly fitted in one person. She grew up following her elder sister closely who passed away in being support to the family. She always wanted to pursue education and believed that Education is the key to excel in life. Even in her early teen age, she used to get up early in the morning and walk for 60 - 90 minutes to reach school.

Though her family couldn't afford bus fare, she still attended typewriting class in both English and Tamil languages from the money she saved by doing odd jobs during her school vacation.

She also educated herself in 'shorthand writing' in both English and Tamil language. In all the little time she got, she somehow used it to empower herself with knowledge. She wanted to pursue her higher studies in college and work as a 'Stenographer' in a company. Her desires were always towards education, hard work and earn money. Seeing the difficulty of the family, she created within her a burning desire to earn and support the family in all means. Also, she saw the suffering of the woman in terms of the unfair treatment they receive for their education, livelihood, and the rejection of the society in considering a girl as more of an expense all throughout life, and the physical difficulty women go through all their life in comparison to man. Also, she disliked marriage and committed herself to the upliftment of her family as her only goal.

By this time, she finished her schooling and wanted to go to college like her brother in order to pursue her dreams. But she was denied further education by her father. Without giving up, she tried to reason with her parents to somehow send her to the college as she wanted to study more. Her father refused saying, "Girls don't need to go to college, this much schooling is enough". She fasted for a week, cried and even pleaded that she would go to college. She even suggested that she would go for part-time work in the evening and she would support her own studies. All she needed was just only her father's permission. Even after all this, nothing worked out and she was not permitted to go to college. Even though she was hurt and felt helpless, she didn't stop and thought of the next step.

Keeping the family situation in mind, she started searching for a job without wasting further time to earn and support the family. She got her first job in a laundry shop's billing section.

Her first salary was 100 rupees. She was very happy with her little earnings and desired to support the family in all possible means. With her hard work, she soon grew in her career. From the laundry shop, she went on to work in various finance companies in the accounts section. She had a competitive edge in 'Typewriting' and 'Short hand' writing, the technical skills required for jobs in those days and which she had learnt earlier came in handy during this part of her work life.

She soon started to supplement her family's income. Due to her shouldering of the family's responsibility, her mother pampered her a lot and regarded her highly. She was always given the best treatment among all, in terms of her preferred food. For example, Amsaveni prefers "dosa" over "idli". As "idli" being cost effective and steam boiled which is given to all the other children and to her father and "dosa" being costly prepared on pan and oil roasted, still her mother prepared only "dosa" for her. Even when she came back from work, she wasn't given any household chores, but was given priority to sleep first without any disturbance. As she was earning, she used to buy clothes for her family members.

On the spiritual side, she was very pious and regularly fasted and performed all rituals to the idols without fail. She even wrote the names of her favorite deity's name more than 108 times (is the norm) whenever she raised any specific prayer request. She also led an exemplary life in her clothing and maintained all the spiritual and traditional standards of her time.

CHAPTER 3

A SOUTH INDIAN MARRIAGE

Marriage of Alwarappan and Amsaveni

1980 till 1982:

> "Marriages are made in heaven, so
> is thunder and lightning"

> -unknown

In those days, great fights and great friendships among women blossoms in the place where they get drinking water. Some of the scenarios happening at that place cannot be expressed in words as they will fall short, but has to be experienced with our eyes and ears. Here, a beautiful friendship blossomed between two women {the late Kalyani Krishnaveni (the late Murugesan Pillai's spouse) and the late Pattamal (the late Sundaram Pillai's spouse)}, in the place where they came to collect drinking water Over a certain period of regular interactions while collecting the drinking water, and while walking back to their homes which were within 200 -300 meters apart, they became close friends to an extent of sharing their personal life's and family issues and sought advice and helped each other.

One day Mrs. Kalyani Krishnaveni was very depressed and looked very sad when she came to fetch drinking water for the home. Mrs. Pattamal who noticed this enquired the reason behind her depression out of concern. Then, Pattamal came to know that Kalyani's third son Alwarappan had quarreled with her so much that day, as he wanted to get married and no one is willing to give their daughter due to his jobless situation. The issue was that he was neither getting any job nor consistently staying in any job due to his short temperament and his bad attitude towards work. He took out all his frustrations on his mother. Kalyani was worried that he being one of the eldest son of the family, was expected to shoulder the responsibility of the family, and instead of taking his life seriously or finding a job to support the family, he was frustrated that his mother was not getting him married soon. Mrs. Pattamal consoled her friend as much as she could and returned to her home after a while.

The following day Pattamal went to Kalyani's home to talk to her son as she also has a son, and like her son taking the responsibility of the family and supporting her daughters, she thought she could explain and convince Alwarappan to take life seriously. While she was talking to Alwarappan at one moment, he turned towards the wall and shed few drops of tears while explaining his miseries.

Mrs. Pattamal was moved in that instant, and made a decision. She invited a marriage proposal. She said to her Kalyani, "I have four daughters and I'll give one of them to your son as I couldn't see him crying. I understand his situation as I also have a son of his age." When she proposed this, she kept in mind her fourth daughter to be given to Alwarappan, but not Amsaveni (the third) as she was primarily now supporting the family and was not interested in marriage too. I have four daughters and I'll give one of them to your son as I couldn't see him crying.

She came back to her home, spoke to her son. In all the family's decisions, more than her husband, she went to her son. At this time, by his hard work and dedication, her son appeared for the government employment exam after his college graduation. Meanwhile he was working in a jiggery shop as a sales man in Shevapet. As a big blessing to the family, he got a government job in the income tax department as a Junior Officer. He became yet another source of inspiration and support to the whole family. A regular government income was considered a great blessing in those days. Even a saying goes on the government job, "Even if its donkey rearing job, it should be a government job". As how these days, getting a job in IT firm, calls for a great status symbol or a big financial freedom to the family, etc, a government job was treated in such a manner.

Once she told her son of her experiences at Kalyani's home regarding Alwarappan, both the mother and son decided on this and went ahead to Kalyani's home and confirmed the proposal between Alwarappan and Mrs. Pattamal's fourth daughter.

Sooner or later when both the men of the house (Sundaram Pillai and Murugesan Pillai) came to know, this issue blew off the ceiling. Soon both the families were called together to talk on this proposal formally. By this time Kalyani Krishnaveni had enquired around, and found that Amsaveni, the third daughter of Pattamal was a working woman and a very responsible daughter handling the household responsibilities. Alwarappan, being not stable at any job and irresponsible in all ways, will be taken care of, if she gets him married to Amsaveni than to her younger sister.

In the same time, Mrs. Pattamal's husband, Sundaram Pillai who was an astrologer, who also performs pooja to the idols, believes in all good time bad time, etc, said that when the elder daughter (Amsaveni) was there, the younger daughter couldn't be given to marriage. This was immediately seconded and emphasized more by Kalyani Krishnaveni as she was already thinking of getting Amsaveni to be married to her son. The elders decided the marriage between Alwarappan and Amsaveni and came home.

When Amsaveni came to know that she's getting married and the marriage has already been arranged, she felt very discouraged and pleaded with her family members not to get her into this. She was more passionate about work, study and support the family rather than getting married. But being a daughter in a South Indian family, her voice was never heard.

The more she refused, the more she was compelled into this marriage. Her mother told about her friend's son crying facing the wall moved her, but her own daughter crying for not to get her married was not heard. Her mother and her brother both compelled to get her married saying that, after her there were 3 more girls in the family. If she refused to get married now, how will they get the others married bypassing the tradition?

Also they were more concerned as to what the society will talk, a woman not wanting to get married, and her sister's are getting married etc. At one point, she felt that they are considering a girl child as a burden and wanted her to vacate the home in the name of marriage so that the next ones also follow the same, etc. Till the marriage day, she kept crying and expressing her lamentation to the whole family, but her voice fell on deaf ears.

The day 5th December, 1982 arrived for a typical Tamil Marriage. Tamil marriages are not very expensive and extravagant as Tamilians believe in simple living. Tamilians are very particular about their customs and traditions. However, Tamil weddings are attended by distant relatives and friends and hence are held on a large scale. There are many wedding rituals which are observed by them, without which the marriage is deemed incomplete. A large wedding hall was booked for the occasion and decorated with flowers and lights. The date for the wedding was fixed after consulting the Hindu calendar. This marriage was celebrated more lavishly as it was the first marriage in the girl's house out of their home (the second daughter's marriage was conducted in a temple).

Also from Alwarappan's family, this was the first marriage after their migration to Salem. So both the families were very excited, except for Amsaveni. She felt, already her dream to study and educate herself was shattered and so is her dream of working and supporting family. As in both the families, they had many adult children, all of them had invited their own friends and families, and both the families had also invited as many people they knew and the wedding hall was filled.

As per the tradition in many parts of India, the women's side had to provide dowry and also bear the cost of the marriage in full. The dowry for this marriage was decided between the elders. Amsaveni's family was asked to give dowry as follows 1. A gold finger ring weighing 15 grams to the bridegroom and 2. Cash of Rs 2500 and 3. As the bride, she has to wear 24 grams of gold in the form of a chain. This may not seem to be a big dowry at all in the South Indian marriage, as gold and land has to be given in large quantity to the bridegroom along with the other demands the bridegroom's family asks for. The interesting part of the dowry was the "Job Offer to Alwarappan" which was the biggest compromise that Pattamal and Kalyani Krishnaveni, had discussed earlier. As Pattamal's son had got the government job and was already in a respectable position, she told her friend (Kalyani Krishnaveni) that her son would get a job for her son Alwarappan after marriage and not to worry. Because of this reason, the material part of the dowry seemed to be very limited. The cost for the marriage was covered from 2 parts by Amsaveni's family. The first part was that, she was asked to apply loan of Rs. 10,000 from her office where she was working, to cover all the costs of the marriage. The other part of the money came from selling the front part of their house.

If you recollect, when Amsaveni was born, this family had obtained a property from their father's side. Now the front portion, being a very significant part of the home was sold to cover the cost of the gold and money which need to be given in the other part of the dowry. The marriage went on very well except for a dramatic scene happened in the dining hall of the marriage.

In South Indian context of marriage, food plays a very important role. Many marriages have fallen apart in the context of food served during the marriage. The bride's side was held fully responsible for it. The food served in the marriage and the treatment given to the bridegroom's side on the dining table, determines the quality of the bride's family. The positive and negative effect of the food during marriage would be expressed in various social issues in the later part of the bride's life after she went to the bridegroom's family. So in this marriage, there was an insufficient quantity of "idlis" serving due to the excessive crowd.

Alwarappan's father had expressed this in such a way that he slammed the door of the wedding hall and walked off from the marriage at the last moment. The marriage ended in a little less happy way compared to the way it had started. Apart from this, the marriage had a great crowd to bless the couple, lavish ambience and a good feeling across the families.

Alwarappan was happy that he finally got married. Amsaveni was feeling more miserable than before with all the atrocities happening around.

CHAPTER 4

CONCEIVED 5 BUT ONLY 1 SURVIVED

1982 till 1984:

"Marriage is a sacred institution which marks the beginning of a new life for the bride and the groom"

Though it all started very disturbing for Amsaveni, the marriage with an unknown man and a new family seemed to be a positive change in the early days of her married life. Both her in-laws loved her like a daughter. As the family had only one daughter, the daughter in law was given equal importance and respect. There was no discrimination or ill-treatment from the in-law's home from the beginning. Things started settling down after marriage, and now when 'the rubber hits the road' the pressure started accumulating.

So far in her mother's home, Amsaveni has not entered kitchen ever once to cook. She didn't even know how to make coffee. This was not acceptable at her in-law's home, where the mother-in-law expects the daughter-in-law to cook and serve the whole joint family from the very next week after marriage.

This was the first cultural shock for Amsaveni. She explained her mother-in-law, but she refused to accept any excuse. She was given all the house course work like washing clothes, cleaning vessels until she learnt to cook. This seemed to be a "Herculean" task for her, as she had never acquired such skills and was never interested to learn too.

Her father in law, who saw her crying while doing the house hold duties one day stopped and asked her. She explained her position in her mother's home and zero exposure in the kitchen.

As he loved her like his own daughter, he started teaching her how to make tea and coffee. Her mother-in-law who noticed this strictly cautioned her husband not to pamper Amsaveni, since it was a large family and daughter-in-law was expected to work. As Amsaveni mother's home was only 200 meters away.

She used to run at any possible excuse to ask her mother and started sharing everything from the in-law's home to her mother and sisters. Little did she realize that this sharing of information from her in-laws to her family would lead to a huge problem.

As per the Tamil custom, couples who got married would visit all the relatives' homes far and near, in the first month of marriage to seek blessings from them. Not all the relatives were happy that Alwarappan got married without even having a job.

The reason for their surprise is that there were few cousins who were elder than Alwarappan but yet not married, just because they were not in job. Also, another reason is Alwarappan's bride Amsaveni was very beautiful to behold and possessed long hair, which was considered to be a symbol of pride. Many comments were passed in a subtle way. This was expressed almost in all relative's home. At one point, he decided to stop visiting any more families and return to his home as such jealousy talks increased his temper. Apart from this, all seemed to be very comfortable. Amsaveni was happy marrying an innocent and loving husband.

On the thirtieth day of their marriage, during their journey back to Salem, Alwarappan was conversing with Amsaveni telling her that soon all the talks of his relatives would come to an end once he get a job. He told he was just waiting to get back home to meet her brother in order to fulfill the promise he had made. This shook Amsaveni for a minute and she responded "with the promise of gold, cash and other wedding arrangements everything had been provided for, what other promise was still lacking to be fulfilled? and why my brother had to make a promise to you?"

By this time Alwarappan had Amsaveni stepping on his nerves as he could not take a woman questioning him. He always had this male dominating ego even among his own family members and thus in a upset yet frustrated voice told that he married Amsaveni because her mother had promised a "job" through her brother, as he's already working in Government and could use his influence to get him a job soon after the marriage. Amsaveni was surprised as she was totally unaware of this conversation till that time and she was neither told about this by her mother or brother before marriage.

She responded to Alwarappan saying that this was not possible, and not to day dream that her brother would be able to get any job for him. She continued saying, if that was the case, he would have got job for her first and her other sisters by this time. More so in her opinion, getting a job should be a man's primary responsibility and he should not have married her just for a "job offer". As this conversation became a big blow to both of them, Alwarappan's angered tone and temperament had made it even worse. From that bus strip onwards, things went from bitter to worse day by day between them.

Amsaveni was heartbroken that her life was ruined not only because her parents denied her education and got her married without her consent, but also because her husband told that he married her to get a "job". On top of all these, she was not aware that she was given in marriage in such a disgusting manner.

Alwarappan on the other hand, felt betrayed that he was cheated by this family in this new place and as this marriage was the first in their family after their migration, everyone had high hopes on it. Also as his relatives were already ill-treating him due to his jobless situation, he had agreed to this marriage proposal happily as his mother told he would be given a "job" as a dowry from the daughter in law's home. Now both had lost the trust in the marriage and both felt betrayal and deceit. This conversation blew up both the families, as Alwarappan in his furious temper came home and yelled at his mother, and even at a point had hit his mother during the argument. When he got angry, he would not be himself, behave so nastily and didn't bother to use any filthy language or raise his voice. Though otherwise, he was very innocent and did not have any bad habits. Not to deny, his temperament, laziness and unwillingness to work hard had ruined his life gradually before and now this has begun to start affecting his marriage.

First abortion: Meanwhile, Amsaveni became pregnant in the first month of marriage. This came to her understanding only after the third month. Meanwhile on the 30th day of her marriage, things went haywire. The relationships between the families were deteriorating day by day. Once the biggest comfort during Amsaveni's marriage was that they were living within walking distance of each other as her in-laws family was very close. During this time, there were very frequent possibility to outburst anger and emotions between the families. The sisters of Amsaveni started getting involved in the fight and slowly the fights between the families extended even in the streets.

The fights which were initially due to the frustration of not being transparent between the families later blew up in picking up words during the fights and started worsening day by day. The friendship between the two women of both houses (Amsaveni's mother and Alwarappan's mother) sored. In all this, Amsaveni's father was not aware that his wife and son had discussed a "joboffer" component in the dowry part. Later both the families were called by the common elders of the community to have a neutral discussion and bring the fight to an end. The very reason of arranging such discussion was shattered at the end. As in this meeting, Amsaveni's brother declared that he would not be able to get any job for Alwarappan as he was not consistent in any of his previous jobs. He was neither flexible nor adaptable to any work atmosphere in which he worked earlier.

To cite an instance, Alwarappan had previously worked in a few market place jobs like counting the number of rice bags needed to be exported in a truck to a few petty shops.

At some point, the owner of the rice mill wanted him to stand out of the store as the owner behaved indecently with the women helpers inside. He wouldn't tolerate such behaviour and he exposed the owner in front of other customers, by calling him out and exposed his dirty mind. In another shop during the day, as the owner entered the shop with a few clients, he saw the front side of the shop was a little dirty and there were no other helpers except Alwarappan. Hence he told him to sweep the place faster as his clients were approaching. Alwarappan, instead of helping the owner took the account book and threw it in front of the owner and yelled at him saying, "Don't you know how to respect a Graduate? I'm working at your shop as an accountant not as a sweeper", and immediately in front of his owner and the clients, he walked out of the shop. This embarrassment made the owner to pass around the news to all his contacts in the market and in no time, the news had spread across all the shop and job firms nearby. Alwarappan, knowing this got even more angry and frustrated. In his anger, he said that he never wanted to take salary for the previous 28 days that he worked for him and came home.

Amsaveni's brother cited the damaged face value of Alwarappan in the market place and washed his hands off him, saying he couldn't find any jobs for him. He insisted that, it was supposed to be Alwarappan's duty as a man to find a job and take care of the family. That day marked a great rift between the two family relationships, and this news spread like a wild fire across the place.

It was at this time that Amsaveni felt the symptoms of pregnancy and hated the very concept to the core. She didn't reveal this to her husband, or to both the families. She kept boggling at the thought of her current situation - just two months after marriage. The situation in her newly married life was completely shattering and she was much fearful and anxious of the new life in her womb. Looking at the economic situation and the day by day degrading relationships between the families, led her to the only decision of aborting the child in the womb. She chose the option thinking that by going through with this, she would have saved the new life from going through any misery. She researched some methods to do it and she approached clinics. No doctor recommended her to abort since it was her first pregnancy and the fetus was growing healthily. Even though she explained her family situation to a few doctors, they explained that problems occur in married life, and not to proceed with the abortion.

Amsaveni was still, unwilling to continue the pregnancy due to the stressful situations at home. She decided to go a little far away out of her town and finally found a clinic where she opted for abortion. As the clinic was not well equipped and the doctor was not experienced, after the abortion, she had some complications. Nevertheless the first fetus of this marriage was crushed to death sometime in the third month of conception.

Second abortion: She hoped things would become better as she took the initiative on her parent's behalf and found a job for her husband in a finance company through her contacts. Alwarappan couldn't agree to the job as he felt that a woman getting a job for the man was beneath a man's dignity to accept it. Though Amsaveni had tried to convince him many times, Alwarappan felt that it was inferior for a husband to get such help from a wife.

Even at this point, he was not feeling inferior that he didn't find any job by himself to make him look better. Later Amsaveni approached her mother-in-law to explain to her son regarding the job which she can get for him, and with her support, she finally convinced her husband to take up the job. After this, things seemed to work out. By now, Amsaveni conceived for the second time in 1983, a couple of months after first abortion.

This time, she wanted to tell to the family but was not sure about her husband's consistency in the job. She was already hearing complaints from her husband on a daily basis about the manager not being good, more work, and referring back to the fact that this was why he didn't accept a job using a woman's help. Due to her improper abortion the first time from an inexperienced clinical setting, one day when she was at home doing the house hold duties, she felt something dropping out of her lower abdomen and felt severe pain.

As no one was at home, she herself rushed to a far-off hospital instead of a nearby one, fearing that if the family comes to know she would be questioned on why she didn't reveal till that time. The doctor enquired about her in detail and found that due to her first abortion, the baby was getting deformed due to complications in the uterus; hence she had to forcefully abort the baby. Time was not left for her to decide as she delayed this enough and her condition was getting worse.

By this time, she was missing from home and her mother-in-law started searching for her, enquiring near and far if they met Amsaveni that day. Meanwhile, the doctor strictly told Amsaveni that she has to go for this abortion before it reaches the point where her life would also be at risk? Hence, fearing the current situation and being overcome by the guilt of the first abortion, she went ahead for the second abortion. Now the fetus was crushed to death without any choice from the mother.

By the time she had completed this abortion it was getting late and she had went home at the earliest and as expected, the whole family was waiting at the entrance. Also the news had spread to Amsaveni's mother's home which was nearby. After questioning her about her whereabouts, both the families came to know about her abortion and the background scenario. As the saying goes, "Misfortune never comes alone" and in Amsaveni's life, misfortune had its permanent place.

Option - Divorce or Child: Both the families considered child birth a blessing and it was quite obvious in the number of children both the families had. Little did their children know that because of many siblings and with a menial income, the family was struggling a lot to meet the daily needs. Ironically, this is the time the Government began conducting awareness campaign on family planning and controlled pregnancy etc.

Now, at this situation, the families returned to fighting after Amsaveni's abortion. Alwarappan's instability in his job and both the families' children every day encountered a fighting scene in either home. In both the families interpretation of the root cause was quite different. Not providing the "job offer" which was promised as per the dowry accepted; was the triggering and sustaining point of fight in Alwarappan's family.

Since their son-in-law was so unstable in his job, their daughter had to work and make ends meet – was the basis of the fight at Amsaveni home. In this entire scenario's Alwarappan expressed his anger by blaming Amsaveni and her family day in and day out. Amsaveni was already feeling guilty of crushing the first child under abortion as she decided that move and the second one was forced to be crushed because of the complications due to the first abortion; she was internally going through a disturbing mindset as she did all of this keeping in mind that the new life should not be part of this great struggle which is happening out due to no peace in the families.

All fights needs to come to an end. This fight also came to an end with two options from Alwarappan's family, as the bridegroom's family always has the upper hand in the Tamil community. Knowing all the complaints on their son's job and nature, Alwarappan's family had agreed to this marriage on the dowry terms of getting a permanent job for him, which Amsaveni's family failed to do until now. Amsaveni, who was expected to birth the heir of the family and enrich the generation, had decided on her own to abort the child without anybody's consent including her husband's and she had failed to perform the duties of a wife. Hence given the option to either conceive a child that year, or get divorced from their son. The bridegroom's family was so worried that their generation wouldn't carry on, won't last without a child born to him and they can get him married a second time to any village girl from their community.

Having an heir seemed to be the priority, than providing the heir a protective, peaceful family environment and economic security. Now the bride's family was startled at this decision as they have daughters following Amsaveni, and in that culture if any issue like this happened in any family, the other daughters may not get married as the elder one had been divorced; there was a 'stigma' attached to this. Nevertheless, they also didn't want Amsaveni to struggle with that family. Now, for the first time but at a very bad timing, they gave the option to Amsaveni and told her to decide for her life. What a tragic point to decide for a bride – on one side it was her dream to support her family and sisters at all times, and on the other side she had to divorce her husband because he was not willing to find a stable job.

Having thought hard, she came up with a bold decision with a supporting argument. She said that she will never go in for divorce as it will impact her family name and moreover, she hasn't committed any mistake in order to go through one. Her point of argument was that this situation has risen because of her husband's incapability to find a job or sustain it but even before this situation, she was earning and supporting the family and hence she will not divorce her husband. Secondly, for the child, she accepted that because of her decision due to her valid reasons though it may not sound convincing that the first abortion occurred, but if the next conception happens, she in all her capacity would protect and bring it out.

Not only that, she proceeded with a recommendation stating that she preferred to go out and start a nuclear family and would not be influenced from either of the families. This was a very bold step from any lady from that community, but Amsaveni had taken this as the option was given to her at the tragic point.

Though the idea was welcomed by her mother's family, the groom's family refused to accept it. They said that, if she insists, they can allow her to be nuclear inside the family itself; she would be given a room in the house and from cooking to washing to all maintenance would be done by her separately but still as a daughter-in-law of the home, she has to support the family by her income and doing the house-hold duties for the larger family also. She agreed without any choice as her husband was not very supportive of her and he was still in his own set of ideals.

Birth of the third Child amidst dreadful difficulties: So Amsaveni and Alwarappan began living 'nuclear' in a joint family. It seemed very strange and more stressful than usual.

But at least this much had happened and her voice had been heard to some extent. Now as the days went by, no symptom of pregnancy nor were there any positive feelings in the family.

By now, Amsaveni's family had slowly became less involved in the family matters of Amsaveni and started ignoring her visits to their home. They expressed no interest to indulge in her in-law's family matter, as no one was motivated to go any step further with her husband's family. Understanding that, Amsaveni also gradually stopped going to her mother's home though it was just 200 metres away. Since she was at work, a major portion of her time was already occupied, and when she returned home, the household chores awaited her now in double portion – one for her nuclear family and the other from her mother-in-law for the joint family. She started to function like a machine, getting up early in the morning, doing her household work, preparing food for her and for her husband, and going to work till late in the evening, and soon afterwards, returning to work for the joint house and by the time she finished work it was already midnight. Her work was not over, as she has to satisfy her husband's desires, and unlike many other men he was more interested in physical intimacy than the emotional intimacy with his spouse.

As the time went by, the option given by the bridegroom's family was reminded time and again in a very subtle manner at any given situation. Things looked much worse for Amsaveni as all were giving her a tough time. Amsaveni was concerned – "what if I don't get pregnant due to the two prior abortions?" This very thought gave her sleepless nights. She started enquiring among her friends and the doctor's didn't give much hope about the next pregnancy – they weren't sure as the uterus which had gone through two forced abortions, thereby crushing the natural child birth would be ready for the next one.

Adding to that, Amsaveni had taken all the astrological papers of hers and her husband's birthdays to five to six astrologers. This has opened another can of worms. As she was checking the astrology papers of her husband, more than one astrologer had asked whether her father was alive. This question startled her.

When she asked for explanation, they all said in the same manner that for this astrological sign and star, they should marry a girl from a fatherless home or else as per Alwarappan's sign, the father-in-law will soon die. She couldn't believe her ears and reconfirmed with few more astrologers but the fact remained the same. She was more worried about her own father (Sundaram Pillai) now than about herself. But things were not clear to her; the astrology papers which her husband's family had given for the marriage should have revealed this.

When she found out that the papers given to her family during the marriage were not the original papers, she felt being deceived. She went ahead to seek clarification from her mother-in-law who was already fuming in anger due to the previous two abortions. Amsaveni's questioning had added more fuel to the fire, but the truth was revealed that Alwarappan's family has changed the original astrological papers fearing that no one will give their daughter to their son in marriage, and if his astrological papers states only a fatherless girl as an eligible bride, then it may take even more time to search for a suitable bride. Moreover in this case, Alwarappan was restless to get married soon and also the proposal came voluntarily from Pattamal - the bride's side.

Now Amsaveni came to know the truth, but she couldn't seek any support from her family as they were gradually departing from her already and this news may shatter them even more.

Adding to it, the news of a fatherless daughter as a requirement would startle the family even more.

But Amsaveni's questions to Alwarappan's family had led her to more troubles, as no in-law's family would like to get exposed of their deliberate act from a daughter-in-law. Now the point had come, that because she was working, started living independently and had started questioning about the astrology papers etc. They have to think of some reason to shut her mouth.

So the talk of she being 'barren' became the hot topic in and around the family. The embarrassment a woman go through on hearing her being barren is not less than killing her slowly with painful words as sharp as a knife.

Moreover, when a woman who was not actually barren but productive and had babies, and actually went through forced abortion and later being labelled 'barren' was even more dreadful and pathetic. With all those painful stings, she continued her search with the astrologer for "a child blessing".

Every astrologer she visited gave a big list of things to do – to buy, to fast, to meditate, to do this that. She did all of them sincerely.

Some of the tasks include bathing yourself with buckets of water and rolling on the outskirts of the temple, eating the food on sand instead of plate (weird though yet true), fasting every alternate days for 3 - 4 deities. Others included writing few deities name in a note book more than 108 times as one session and repeat the same 10 - 12 times in a day, going to a particular temple once a week and preparing a garland with tiny paper-pieces with the Deities' name on it. To imagine, that Amsaveni had to do all this amidst all her daily house chores, office work and along with the enmity she started creating due to her questioning of the truth.

In spite of doing all the above duties so sincerely, she didn't get any symptoms of pregnancy at all. Further she went ahead to seek the guidance from a well renowned priest who was also a famous astrologer. Looking at all the papers, he asked her to find some answers from both the family members for the questions he had asked. The outcome was more challenging than all the above scenarios.

The priest had declared that Alwarappan had a curse from the Snake King (cobra), it seemed that one day in their old home, a cobra was found between the bricks of their house and he had attempted to kill it, but had left it half dead. This was considered a serious curse because the 'snake/serpent' was worshipped as one of the holy deities, and in situations like that, you should have either killed the snake completely or you should not even attempted to kill it, leaving it midway was considered to be a curse, and a sure revenge from the half-dead snake. In addition to this, Amsaveni's father also was told that he had the similar curse from Cobra.

Here in this matter, the previous generation of Amsaveni's father used to be the landlords of a community, and while acquiring one of the lands they had demolished the Snake temple (the usual ones you see in a cone shape built by ants) and had built a house in the same place later. In a very strange timing, Alwarappan and Amsaveni's family had come under the curse of the snake. The priest told that this was more dreadful and there was no great remedy for this curse.

In addition, this curse mainly attacks the heir of the family, from its womb. He added that that may be the reason why the situation was so bad from the beginning of the marriage and both the fetus/babies conceived were crushed in the womb itself. Amsaveni broke down even further as things were out of control, and she has done nothing to deserve this curse. Just because she was born to the family who had done such an act or sin, she was now in the situation to pay for it.

On the other hand, her husband who left the cobra undead had to bear the curse too. So she started reading all the holy books that her father used to read; all what the temple priest had told to read just to find a redemption plan. She spent more time reading and trying to find somewhere if there was a solution for this curse, a hope to be relieved from the curse of sin. The more she read, the more fearful things she found out that 'Karma' or the 'deeds' what you do determines how the supreme power will respond to you. You have to do more good works/deeds, be more pious and increase the level of your 'Punyah' or purified work in order to reduce the 'pappah' or sin that had been bestowed on the individual or the family.

It was more of a man reaching out to the Supreme Being's help through his hard work, self-righteousness, good works, etc, and still it was not a complete remedy for the sin. In some places she read, "Complete Destruction" from the Supreme Power to those who had committed sin, and the revenge from the Snake Deity was more fearful and trembling. She went back to the priest in an even more confused state than before. The priest after so many rituals had told her a remedy. She had to calm down the anger of the Snake Deity, to get some grace to be out of the severity of the curse and suggested two things - 1) She has to get up early morning and take a cup of fresh milk and non-boiled egg and go to a similar Snake temple which her ancestors had demolished, and pour the milk and the egg in that temple without fail for a number of days. She has to start this after 30 days and particularly on a full moon day. 2) As her husband had beaten the serpent and had left it half dead, the severity of the revenge would be more, and to ease that snake's anger, if at all she bears a child, she should name the baby after the serpent as Cobra King (Naga Rajan) if it's a boy, or Cobra Queen (Naga Rani) if it's a girl. The more the people call the name, the less severe the curse could be after some years.

By this time, Amsaveni was mentally prepared to do anything just to get a baby child, in order to clear the name 'barren' and to come out of her guilt of having crushed two fetus' in the womb itself.

But as a strange surprise, even before she started to do the first suggested remedy, she conceived and could feel the symptoms of pregnancy. She couldn't believe this at all. She went more than once to check with the doctor, her mother-in-law and the other elders of the community couldn't believe that the conception was true. To her stunning surprise, YES she conceived, before she started doing the remedy or any other ritual. Her joy had no leaps and bounds. She felt this incident as her 'rebirth' as because of this, no one would anymore call her 'barren' and the in-laws family cannot force the option of divorce anymore. She was full of joy and merrier than ever before.

She was equally joyful to inform the news to her father's family but she didn't get a great response from there, but just a sigh of relief that now she won't have the option of being sent back home since she was no longer barren. Even though this response was unexpected by Amsaveni, she was more happy than anything that she conceived after all this struggle and uncertainties.

9 months of pregnancy and 9 ways of disruption:

1. The first month of conception was full of joy and happiness for Amsaveni, not so much with the families as they were not so excited, neither was they sad nor disturbed. But no one had accompanied her to the doctor or given any suggestions on the do's and don'ts during the pregnancy. Nevertheless, things went forward without much stress in the first and second month apart from the normal symptoms like morning sickness, vomiting sensation etc.

   • By the end of second month, the first obstacle was thrown at her. This was when she went to her mother's home for some work and she happened to see the second son of her elder sister at some point. The time she had seen him, seemed to be a bad omen for her sister's son, because it was believed that if a pregnant lady sees her elder sister's child, it is a bad omen for the child, especially if it's a son. Though this belief seemed to be meaningless, the elder sister started talking or rather slowly pestering her to abort the baby as it was not good for her son. The belief goes on, that from the time this pregnant lady had seen the sister's child, the fetus will take the strength of the child and the sister's child will fall sick and gradually loses its health.

- Firmly adding to the belief, the number of days Amsaveni was at her mother's home (a week), and her sister's son had fallen terribly ill with no symptoms of physical illness. Also the elder sister enticed her to abort the baby for her child's good health sake and she will support her during any family problems or financial problems, hinting that her husband was not at any job properly and that they don't need a child so early. This pressurized her so much that at one point, Amsaveni had to get back to her in-law's house rather than staying in her mother's home.

2. In the third month of her pregnancy, when she came back to her in-law's house, the hectic life had commenced again. She was still working at home and out of home. The in-law's house was not as happy as the daughter in law's family did not follow the custom of buying gold ornaments for their son-in-law due to the baby's conception. This is due to the sore relationship between the families. More so, the whole conception was not very welcoming as it came after some bitter experiences. At this point, neither the fetus was not getting enough nutrition nor Amsaveni was not having enough bed rest.

Physically she was straining herself in work and in her house chores. Mentally she was unhappy due to the deteriorated relationship between the two families. Just like any other pregnant women she too had the desires to eat good food according to her taste and take enough rest and sought the support of her husband. But she didn't get either one of them. This had actually led her to over straining, finally leading her to faint quite often at the work place. The doctor was not happy with the inadequate way; the fetus was being taken care of.

3. When the situation was explained to her husband, he went ahead and argued with his mother, about why his wife was not given any care when his other brother's wife was given all the care and support. Annoyed at this tone and words, his mother told him of how he has started listening to his wife and creating issues with her; and from now on, he could take his wife and live somewhere else.

    The situation got worse after his argument with his mother and finally led Amsaveni and Alwarappan leaving the house and finding an individual accommodation at one of their friend's place.

4. Now going through such emotional atrocities, Amsaveni started cursing herself to be to be born as a female rather than a male, where the girl from her birth to death has to depend on one or another, her freedom completely trapped, neither is her voice heard or her desires met, and all considering the girl to be a burden in the home and treated only as a child-bearing machine and to dance according

to other's desires. So she determined to pray more fervently to have a boy than a girl, as deep in her heart the experiences she had went through had really made her to feel that a female child was a curse and a male child was a blessing. Also in those days, the daughter-in-law was treated differently if she gives birth to a female child instead of a male child. So her prayers began so vigorously and she started to adhere all that the temple priest had told which included various ceremonials, rituals, offering etc.

5. To make matters worse, the husband once again in his temper had lost the job and returned home jobless which was a terrible blow for Amsaveni during her pregnancy. She was already going to work, getting up early to collect water from a far-off place and doing all the house chores, where her husband at this time lost the job and sought to pack his food for lunch and go to the library to read books rather than find a job.

6. Very often an accident occurred in the market place when Amsaveni was returning from work. The traffic in the market place varied at different times during the day. Given the busy traffic, the truck always were at low speed levels, but there were a few truck drivers, wanting to show off their driving skills, would deviate and drive in the small street between houses, by taking such shortcuts and drive fast to their destination. In their attempt to perform such stunts, few of the mothers and pregnant women would most likely lose their lives. Twice, Amsaveni was narrowly about to be hit by a truck and she somehow managed to save her. At one point she

crossed the road and seeing the truck coming; she hurried and fell on top of a stone face. At once, she rushed to the hospital thinking that her little baby was dead, but fortunately it was alive.

7. The Baby shower used to be a ritual for every mother especially in their first pregnancy. But neither Amsaveni's nor Alwarappan's family had done this for her, as both were not much interested in her happiness. Amsaveni's family was fuming in anger due to Alwarappan's attitude towards his job dropping behaviour. From the in-law's side, they were upset that Amsaveni was independent and was not subjected to her mother-in-law's administration. Hence both families were not interested in giving her a baby shower. Every woman delights to be pampered and given courteous treatment during pregnancy but the baby shower was not experienced by her.

8. Amsaveni was questioning herself as to why such misfortunes continue in her life. In spite of being pious and performing all her religious rituals and seeking help from all their deities every day. Working tirelessly among all odds and sourcing income, yet being hated by both the families. Yes she was aware, that her one act of abortion for an authentic reason leading to another unexpected abortion was a grave mistake. But with a pestering husband who was continuously unstable at his work and complained always that her family had cheated him on the job –offer, she was helpless. In spite of all this, she continued to be pious and sincere in adhering to her rituals and fasting, writing deity names and

chanting them continuously and devoted herself to pray for a male child. She was definitely not willing to see a female child in her womb. She used to pray telling that if the baby is born as a girl, she would rather commit suicide and die than seeing the pain of having a daughter. Most of her pregnancy period was never a happy one as nothing turned out well for her.

9. Finally, one Saturday day morning on November 1984, when the whole of India was mourning the assassination of the late Mrs. Indira Gandhi, the then prime minister of India, Amsaveni was getting ready to her work and suddenly she felt the contractions of labor pain. She called the mothers from both sides, but none had turned out to be with her and each one telling her to take the other (Pattamal telling her to take Kalyani and vice versa).

She was crying in pain that even during her labour she has no one to help her. Also, her husband was not at home that time. In her desperate state, she caught an autorickshaw and went by herself for delivery in a Government hospital, where pregnancy will be taken care off at a low cost and most of the times without any charge.

She experienced the labor pain at around 8 am and by 8.30 am she reached hospital, and she was taken to labor ward by 8.45 and most blissfully without any additional pain and just in a matter of 10 minutes at 8.55 am, as all her prayers were answered, a baby boy was born to her. Though no one was there from her family to hold her little boy after coming into the world, Amsaveni forgot all her pain, sorrow, depression and was tremendously happy for the second time after her conception and expressed a very big sigh of relief that she gave birth to a boy. Out of all the disruptive disturbances during these 9 months, the little boy survived and as a first miracle, the mother had painless normal delivery. The doctors who attended on her blessed her saying that the normal delivery causes birth pain but in just a matter of 10 minutes, she had given birth without any medical attempt to induce pain or any anaesthesia to operate upon.

Later sometime during mid-1985 and on Feb 1986, Amsaveni miscarried twice. Sadly but more profoundly only one fetus, one baby survived all the 5 conceptions. Only one baby survived all the obstacles of curse, complication of earlier abortions, stress and disruptions during every month of pregnancy. Either voluntarily or involuntarily the other fetus couldn't survive enough to complete their 9-month journey in the womb to come into this world.

Later on the same day, 3rd November 1984 itself, Amsaveni was discharged from hospital, and by that time, both the family members had arrived one after another to see Amsaveni's new little boy. Earlier, as the priest had cautioned, due to the curse of snake in the family, her son was named NAGARAJAN (Cobra King). Also, the in-law's side had given another name to the child MURUGESAN, the name of the grandfather. Unlike Alwarappan, the grandfather's name was given to the grandson. Also, the little one was the first heir of the generation. Alwarappan was proud that he became the father of the only grandson in the family and hence the little boy was named as NAGARAJAN alias MURUGESAN.

CHAPTER 5

SUICIDE ATTEMPT IN 1 YEAR AND 3 MONTHS

November 1984 till February 1986: The next 15 months had seen startling life changing events in all three lives, Amsaveni, Alwarappan and the little boy Nagarajan. Till a week after the birth of Nagarajan, Amsaveni stayed at her in law's home but preferred to go to her mother's home for hers and the little boy's care. Currently, she was not given that expected care from her mother-in-law's home. Also, having given that birth amidst all tough situations, she was already emotionally and physically drained. Hence, she preferred her mother's care at this moment and she did express it to her in-laws. This view did not sit well with her mother-in-law at all. Since she desired to go to her mother's home, she requested her husband, but there was no positive response. When her mother came to visit her the following day, she expressed her concern to be with her and cried to take her home with her. Her mother went to speak to Kalyani on a friendly note to explain the need of her daughter to be cared for after her pregnancy. There was not much acceptance from Kalyani which angered her mother. So Pattamal took a forced decision – she told Amsaveni to pack her belongings and come home with her. Though Kalyani didn't give the permission and neither was Alwarappan very supportive of this, she went with her mother to her home which was very near.

This act brought up the ego issues and considered as disrespect to the groom's home. At one point Kalyani said, "If you don't come back home in a day's time, you'll never step into this house again". Amsaveni was seeking guidance from her mother. She backed her up and said, "I'll handle Kalyani, you go to work from here and we'll take care of the child. You need to be taken care of and here neither your mother-in-law nor anyone was taking care of the little boy. Your husband is only interested to sleep with you but has no intention to be of any help to you". So Amsaveni stayed at her home and she didn't go to her in-laws place.

"Happiness is not a destination. It is just the moment, but even that passes away after few minutes and leaving us in a state of search for the next such moment"
– Edwin Paul Franklin

The happy moment in Amsaveni's life was that she delivered a boy as her heart's desire but in just a matter of a few weeks, the families were separated for a trivial reason. Now Amsaveni was staying at her mother's home and going to work, and the little boy was taken care by her mother and sisters. But on the other side, anger and frustration was mounting on her husband's home as she walked out of their house disrespecting them. Time and again they were sending threats that they will get their son married off, she would never walk into their house again, they would disown her etc. But Amsaveni's mother and sisters backed her up telling her not to bother up those threats as she was a mother now of their only grandson, so all the threats would not come to pass.

Amsaveni continued with her work but one day while she was still at work, her little boy had severe stomach upset, and the family had taken him to the hospital. When the news reached Amsaveni, she hurried off to the hospital. However, her in-laws also heard the news and they too arrived at the hospital.

When they reached to see the little boy, Amsaveni's sisters who were there had refused them to see or take the baby. At that moment, Alwarappan was told by his mother to remove his shirt, wrap the baby and take him to their home by force. When Amsaveni reached the hospital five minutes later and heard the whole situation, she cried and ran to her mother-in law's home.

She just wanted to see her little boy and what had happened to him. Her little boy was just sixty days old at this time. The whole street had come to know about this and all were gathered around both the homes. Alwarappan's mother sternly told her that she would not allow Amsaveni to step inside their home, and that they would take care of the baby as he was the heir of their family. The whole family of Amsaveni was on the streets and apart from her, all others were shouting at each other. The scene was very disruptive. Alwarappan and his family didn't want to hear from any of them or the elders around. They withstood their decision. The baby was given powdered milk instead of mother's milk. Every day for almost a week Amsaveni used to stand in front of their house and plead but no one from the house would lend an ear.

When her breast milk couldn't be drunk by her son, she had to forcefully suppress it, almost killing her physically and emotionally.

She was not even allowed to see the child who was sleeping in the cradle. All the men folks of the house standing at the command of their mother and Alwarappan had this sense of accomplishment that he had snatched the baby from Amsaveni's family. He thought that this was the lesson for Amsaveni to listen to her husband and in-law's and never disobey their commands.

Days passed by, the problem pestered and the baby was not given breast milk after the first sixty days when he was with his mother. Amsaveni sought help from her family to go and convince her in-law's family as she just wanted to see the baby. But it was their turn for payback, when any one from Amsaveni's family came for a peace talk or to ask for the baby, they showed no respect and didn't allow them into the house, and such a hostile environment had again called for a big fight again between the family members. At one point certain words from both the families triggered the other and it got physical. Already three weeks without even seeing her baby, Amsaveni was going insane. After continuous fighting, one day Amsaveni family told her that they couldn't go and get humiliated in front of her husband's home time and again. Since it was her child, she had to go and deal with the matter.

That day with all the frustration and depression mounting on all sides, Amsaveni had gone to her husband's home to request permission to see the baby at least once. Instead, she was told to leave their premises at once. Nothing could turn their stony hearts to hear the cry of Amsaveni. This was the revenge her mother-in-law was looking for. At one point, Amsaveni lost her patience, came out of their premises, took two hands full of sand, blew it on the family and cursed them saying, "From my womb's pain I curse you that this family will never have any more male child and all children ever born will be females, then you will understand the cry of a female for her child." She also cursed the attitude of the family and their stony heart and repeated this till she was exhausted.

She didn't go home but went to the nearby temple, to question the deity whom she was serving all these days to answer her. The situations she was facing, one after another, pain after pain, fear after fear, depression after depression, she wanted answer from the deities. She was crying her heart out in front of them to look into her situation if they had eyes or ears to come and give her some answer and a hope to live. The idols couldn't respond, neither any of the people who were believed in those deities could respond to any of her questions. The whole night she was crying and questioning her own situation.

She was harboring thoughts of killing herself after seeing all this, being totally helpless and cornered from all sides. "To live or not to live" was the profound question in her mind. The thought started here as Susanna Kaysen, mentioned

"Suicide is a form of murder - premeditated murder. It isn't something you do the first time you think of doing it.
It takes getting used to.
And you need the means, the
opportunity, and the motive"

The following day again she went to her in-law's house early in the morning and started to plead. At this time, her father-in-law came to her rescue. He felt that this girl had suffered enough, amidst other resistance from his wife and others, he had to let her in to see her infant. She fell at his feet and ran to see the infant after almost fifty days. Words couldn't express the pain, agony, depression, mixed emotions, betrayal and cry for help of that mother who was refused her infant baby who was snatched from her for fifty days.

She took the baby and kissed him all around and was overwhelmed with joy. She just couldn't control her emotions on seeing the baby and didn't want to leave that place. But it didn't last long enough when her mother-in-law had said, "We'll only allow her to see the baby but not to stay in this home. She can come to see the baby every day and do the chores, but should not dream of staying here for more than few hours." Amsaveni was ready to do anything just see her little son and agreed to it.

Now when she came to her own home, different things are shaping up with her family members stating that she had entered her husband's home without asking them. Thus the whole family was embarrassment by her deed, the whole community was looking down on their family due to her marriage, and today she had stepped into their home and has dishonored their family even more. All of them at once stated that they would no longer involve in her family matters. It's was up to her to leave the house as soon as possible as the family has other daughters that had to get married, and they couldn't support her life when they were not respected. Amsaveni had kept all these words in her heart, but she couldn't respond at that situation.

The few hours spent every day in visiting her infant son marked the happiest moments for Amsaveni. By this time she lost her job due to her constant absence, ever since the day her son was snatched from the hospital. But she had to support the family, since her husband was still not working. She started searching for a job, and with her past work experience, very soon she got another job in a company as a personal assistant to the manager. The few hours of visiting her little boy every day very slowly changed to staying with him for two full days in a week and later she was allowed to stay in their home but separate from the joint family. Alwarappan was again found a job by Amsaveni at the Salem Cooperative society in the Pharmacy section. When the baby was 6 months old, Amsaveni with her husband and son had moved a little far from both the parents' home for the first time after marriage (a journey time of thirty to forty minutes).

Always, the time spent by a couple with each other brings out clear communication or an attempt to understand each other's desires and feelings and results in better harmony. Amsaveni and Alwarappan had slowly tried to forgive each other and forget all that had happened between them and their families, and decided to start a new life once again along with their baby.

The next four to five months went on smoothly, and both tried to cope up with each other, and the family started to settle down slowly.

Amsaveni and Alwarappan with their little boy

As both of them were going to work, a babysitter was hired, but he refused to take care of the baby as he was under aged. Amsaveni had to convince the caretaker explaining her situation of her husband going to work, and they have moved away from their parents' home, and were trying to stand on their own. But the caretaker insisted that the small boy was just beginning to crawl and this was the time that the parents need to spend time with the kid, and henceforth leaving the baby with a baby sitter at this young age was not a best suggestion.

However, empathizing with another working woman, the baby sitter finally accepted to babysit the 10 months old infant. The daily routine of the three was something like this – Amsaveni has to wake up early in the morning at around 4 am and walk a mile to fetch drinking water from a well. Once she comes back by 5 am and start the morning household chores, like cleaning and watering the front side of the house, put 'Kolam' in front of the house (Kolam is a form of painting that is drawn using rice powder/ chalk/chalk powder/white rock powder often using naturally/ synthetically colored powders in Tamil Nadu, it is widely practised by female Hindu family members in front of their homes). Then prepare breakfast and lunch for her and her husband. Make all the necessary arrangement for the baby like milk, baby food etc. and prepare the bag for the baby sitter. Once the baby woke up, she would ready the baby and give powdered milk (after the 50 days of separation the baby got used to the powdered milk and due to the stressful and depressing moments, she was not able to breastfeed her baby as the milk secretion had stopped).

In the meantime her husband would wake up, get ready for his job, and all three would leave the house by 8 am. First the baby would be left in the care of the babysitter, and then she would be dropped at her work place on a bicycle by her husband, and then he will reach his workplace by 9 am. By 3 pm, she would walk from her office to the babysitter and take the little one home, bathe him and put him to sleep.

Then she would clean the vessels, do the remaining chores and by 5 pm, she would get ready for her part-time job as a tutor in a typewriting institute, (as she had passed out in distinction in both English and Tamil typewriting). She would frequently leave her son with her neighbor till she comes back at 9 pm, and sometimes her husband would come at 8.30 pm and take the baby from there. Once she came back she would cook dinner and by 10 pm, the baby and her husband would sleep.

But she had to wash all the dirty clothes taking them to the nearby well (since it wasn't busy at that time), and return home by 11pm. From 11.30 pm to 4 am was her resting time.

In a few months' time, she conceived again and this time whether she liked it or not, she did not proceed as before but let it live. Unfortunately, in the second month itself due to all her stressful lifestyle, she had a miscarriage and the baby didn't survive. Though she felt very happy with the family being together for the last three months, it was physically and emotionally exhausting due to her non-stop work routine. The thoughts of being born as a female as a 'curse' grew strongly in her mind as there was no help from her family members. Missing the time with her son/lack of emotional support from her husband used to depress her. At times like this, she thought whether it was worth living going through all this every day, Nevertheless she pressed on; hoping there will be a light at the end of the tunnel, as she was still pious and fasted for all the female deities of her religion.

She prayed without ceasing to give her more strength to face life, and she was still praying to find some hope or an answer from a supreme power. She was searching for the purpose of her life amidst all this, and she was still trying to match her good deeds with the past evil deeds in order to reduce the curse which was upon her family, as repeatedly mentioned in her religious books.

Now they were nearing to the birthday of their son – twelve months in the struggle of protecting and providing the baby seems to be a great accomplishment for Amsaveni. The baby boy turned one on November 3, 1985. She arranged for a small celebration at her in-law's home from her savings every month. As her son was an important part of her life, she wanted to celebrate his first birthday in a grand manner.

The party was attended by all her colleagues, her husband's colleagues, her relatives, her husband's relatives and all the other friends. Little did she know that not all came to celebrate but some to criticize as well. Some of them were pulling Alwarappan aside, and asking him about how he could stay in this job for such a long time. Others criticized the arrangements made for the celebration stating that, this was too much of a show off since they both are working and wanted to spend more.

On the other hand, some were commenting that because she was little educated and a working woman she could go out of the house, didn't need to live with her in-laws and do all of this as a free woman. Some wanted to wait and see how long she could continue like this. They made her to realize,

"If you expect the world to be fair with you because you are fair, you are fooling yourself. That's like expecting the lion not to eat you because you didn't eat him"

Her mother, father and her sisters were really happy to see her successful life amidst all that she went through, and living as an example of a strong and overcoming woman. Also her father-in-law and few of her husband's brothers genuinely appreciated the initiative she took in bringing the family together, despite knowing how their own son was. Whether people appreciated her or not, she did what was right as she always wanted the family to be together and hearing all such criticism had really made her depressed, but still she continued to be good to those who were around her all the time.

From this day, exactly three more months later, the events that took place in Amsaveni's life were quite taxing and more stressful than in the twenty seven years of her life. The three most striking scenarios follow: You might have heard people saying, that just before they finished facing one problem the next one is just waiting for its turn, and before they get out of one, the next one was already putting them down. After the birthday party, both Amsaveni and Alwarappan were back to their routine tasks. The managers from her part time and full time job, who had attended the birthday party at Amsaveni's home, had seen the active young lady outside office on that day. They also observed her husband's behaviour and family's situation.

Evil thoughts crept in their minds, and just the very next day when she went back to work, her manager had told her to stay back and work overtime as he wanted to complete some project. Initially Amsaveni didn't take any notice that something was coming. She stayed back until 8 pm and had to skip the part time work for that week in order to complete the work the manager gave her. A few days later, on one evening, he asked about her personal life, her family members, appreciated the birthday party, enquired about her husband. Though she tried to avoid giving details to his questions, she started to realize that she was getting trapped by his queries to know her family and economic situation.

Meanwhile, the manager from the part time job started noticing her absence, had sought an explanation over the phone. She explained that due to her other work's extending hours she couldn't come that week, but would come to work like before from next week. He was waiting for her to come next week, and wanted to enquire more about her family than about her work.

Next week, he also started expressing his 'pseudo-concern' to show his sympathy on her family's situation. At times, he was also telling her on how he wished that he could have had a spouse like Amsaveni who was so talented, beautiful and responsible, and he slowly started sharing his personal story to her voluntarily. On a couple of occasions, Amsaveni told him right away that she was not interested to hear his personal life story and it was not good for him to share such things with the staff.

Slowly but steadily, her full time job manager was trying his best to make her stay back one week after another – he had offered her overtime continuously and thereby tried to stop her from going to her part time job. Amsaveni, who was already displeased with the part time job manager and his behavior, was considering leaving the job permanently as she could get the same income in her overtime. But one day, her finance company manager started making sexual advances in words and action on her when she was about to leave from office. She was shocked to the core and told him more sternly that she was not there to use her body but her skills only, and this was not expected of him. She also told him that she had respect on him till now and any such behavior will only lead her to quit her job immediately.

But he was persistent; he told her the good life she can have in luxury, job promotion, comfort if she would just accept him to have her in the office after office hours. He was persistent in trying out sweet words to seduce her, reminding her of her family and economic situation. He also told her that this would be a secret affair and no one would know, if she would only co-operate.

Amsaveni couldn't accept this, as she treated her self-esteem and ethics as second only to her life. At one point, she slapped him when he tried to come near to molest her. From that day onwards she refused to stay back and do any overtime; she came in when all other staff were present and left along with everyone, just to protect herself from him.

During this time, she continued to go to part time job in the evenings as she stopped the overtime shift. This had paved way for the part time job manager to rekindle his feelings towards her. A little later in the week he started again, reverted to the same storytelling about his wife and his dissatisfying married life. Now Amsaveni was even more cautious than before as she was just exposed to a similar incident in her full time job. She was thinking of quitting the part time job once for all, as she understood by now, the motives of the manager and where he was heading.

From that day, things were not easy at work, as she refused the advances of both her managers. Holding on to her ethics and self-esteem, she was still trying to swim against the current. It was not easy for her to share this with her husband, knowing that he was a short tempered person; he may only end up in shouting or telling her to stop working. But looking at his capacity to support the family or to provide for their son, she couldn't take that step. Still, at the back of her mind, she decided to leave the job once she feels confident that her husband was steady at his work.

On the other end, her husband who was working a little longer than a few months at the Cooperative society in the pharmacy division, had a big shock in his office place. Being very ignorant and not smart at the work place, he had been taken for a ride. Just as in the stock market where the previous sales persons provide fake accounts and false stock update, thereby selling the product out for a lower rate, Alwarappan, who was supervising them was expected to be prudent in finding this out and bringing it to the attention of the management, was not sharp enough to do that. He was carried away by the words of his sales people and was just maintaining the records submitted by them without cross checking daily. During the yearly audit, this came to light, but more than the sales person being caught, the supervisor Alwarappan was caught in the enquiry. During the enquiry, the sales personnel had told that Alwarappan was aware of it from the beginning and they have done everything under his instruction. Though it was a white lie, Alwarappan was not in a position to fight back or to defend as he was unaware of this until that moment. At the enquiry, he was found to be more incompetent that he was not able to identify this issue at the early stage and was held responsible for the entire dilemma. This led him being fired from the job with the instruction to pay back all the shortage stocks which came up to 20 lakhs of rupees in today's value. Losing his job in less than 6 months, and ending up paying a huge sum of money for no fault of his was a big blow to the family. He came back to home with this message, when Amsaveni was already in the mind set of quitting her job due to the abuse from her managers. She couldn't believe her ears when her husband told her what had happened, but neither could she argue with him knowing his capacity, thereby putting her in a helpless situation. Now when she went to seek guidance from her family members, they saw this more of a burden to them than to the family on whole, and tried to get away from this, the issue was passed between the two families. It was clear that no one wanted to get involved in their problems, knowing Alwarappan's nature and having such a big financial burden. The situation demanded her to apply for a loan from her company at least to keep the ball rolling. But unintentionally, this became more of a fish voluntarily coming inside the net to get trapped. Now one after another, both the managers, even before deciding how much loan they could provide in this situation, more focused on getting her trapped. This went on for a week. In between such helpless situations and no room for hope, it was a part of herself that she wanted to kill: the part that wanted to kill her dragged her into the suicide debate and made every truck, kitchen tools, and petrol and railway track as a rehearsal for tragedy. The thoughts of suicide which earlier originated at the time when she yearned to meet her son a few months ago, resurfaced as her situations became tough to bear.

As there was no positive response from Alwarappan in the enquiry or in providing a deadline to pay back the financial loss to the company, they went ahead to file the case in court, and to add fuel to the fire, the court has sent a notice to Alwarappan to present himself on a given date. A big argument as never before broke out between Alwarappan and Amsaveni, where he still didn't accept the fact that his carelessness was the cause for their losses and neither did he try any means to solve this. Amsaveni, who has been cornered from all sides, was pouring out her frustration and helplessness to seek some sort of hope amidst the situation from her husband and from her family members, but all ended in vain. At times, she thought as Friedrich Rodger

"The thought of suicide was a great consolation: by means of it one gets through many a dark night."

The next day, she went to her mother's home, to leave her son and to be away from her husband for a few days just to recompose herself and to think clearly. The pressure was mounting as the managers were wanted to seduce her; the court's notice was on call for action, her family's didn't want to get involved, and her husband was as ever immature and irresponsible. She battled with her thoughts day in and day out, and she was breaking down internally and externally, as Albert Camus says,

"In the end one needs more courage
to live than to kill oneself"

In the end, she found a way to end her life. Until that point, her only comfort was that her child was a boy and not a girl. He would somehow be taken care of by either family as both loved to see the baby. She had lost all hope in her husband and on either family. Bitter situations are the best opportunity for people like Amsaveni's managers to exploit her by using their power. She came to the point where she thought it would be better to yield to a one time death than to such killing situations one after another. Hence, her mind was only contemplating a successful suicide which demands successful planning and a cool head, both of which are usually incompatible with the suicidal state of mind. Within three months from her baby's first birthday, the three big blows were too much for Amsaveni to sustain further in her endurance, hard work and commitment to keep the family intact. She wanted to make just one but being successful in suicide. She had heard about half attempted and failed suicides, and never wanted to fail in at least attempting it. Hence she planned it very seriously. The pressure was still high from all the ends. She stopped without notice from going to work, and began staying at her mother's place for the baby's sake. She started to set her house in order with whatever was left out, and tried to spend as much time as possible with her little son, talking to him in a language which he won't understand but only her heart understands. Before the final stage of her plan was to be implemented, she arranged to meet her husband in the temple, where earlier she was crying bitterly just to see her son and was questioning the idols about why such things happened. She asked her husband to pick her up for the one last bicycle ride with him. When she met her husband at the temple, she was there till midnight talking to her husband very casually, but not a single word from her depressed and decided thoughts. They had their dinner outside and she was dropped back at her home and bid farewell. She told him that tomorrow she would come home, and asked him to be ready to pick her for work and handed the house key to him.

After the final farewell she went to her home, and as everyone was sleeping by this time, she went and sat with her son who was peacefully sleeping in the cradle. In the next few hours, the most dreadful hour for her life was about to happen.

She decided to jump in the well at their place. It was known to be a deep well and had served the community drinking water. She thought of ending up in the well where she couldn't resurface even if she doesn't die immediately, she would eventually drown since she didn't know swimming. Since she didn't want to fail in her attempt, she gave no option for her to be rescued.

Moreover this well was a common drinking place and was present in the center of their neighborhood. She chose it since she wanted everyone to come to know that a woman who had struggled all her life just for the good of her family, food and shelter had ended her life as she couldn't face it anymore. That day early morning (Feb 1986) at 4 am when everyone was still asleep, she woke up, kissed her little baby for one last time and tried to get out of the house. In the dark atmosphere, she mistakenly stepped on her father's leg, and he woke up and asked who it was. She answered saying that it was her and was going to buy milk (it was customary for women or men go out early in the morning at around 5 am (not 4 am when Amsaveni pointed out) to buy milk at the market, and unlike grocery shops these days, milk was not available everywhere at one's reach.

She decided nothing would stop her, really nothing, not her religious books, chants, fasting, family, husband, son; none would stop her from taking her life. She went to the well which looked even darker than her life, so deep and disturbing!!!

For one last time, she thought about all she went through in her life till that moment, and she felt cursed to go through that. But in the next few minutes, she wanted to end it once and for all. At that moment too, her only happiness was that her child was not a girl, it was enough being a girl in the family and society.

Even at that point, she felt that though her husband and family were in various ways the reason for the troubles she was going through, still no one would take the bold decision which she had taken, because in the end, it was only she that was fighting against every situation and problem all alone, all by herself, with her hard work, knowledge, and with her experience.

She couldn't think no more and here she was at the brink of the well, counted her last few seconds and jumped into the well once for all.

Now, what do you think?

"Did she really want to die?

Did she commit suicide because she just wanted to die?

Can't she still hold on? Can't she be more pious?

Wasn't she bold enough to face the life situations so far?

Wasn't she working hard amidst all exhaustive scenarios and unfulfilled desires till now?

Wasn't she truly genuine and responsible to toil for the betterment of her family at all times?

Wasn't she fighting against the ruthless practices of dowry, abuse and social issues?

Did she yield to the richness and comfort at the cost of her chatity?

Did she let her self-esteem to compromise for any filthy act?

Though both families did not stand with her
till the end, she not battling all alone?

Though Society couldn't protect her, her deities
couldn't come when she cried for help,

Though her husband was not bothered
about her emotions or feelings, wasn't she
still pressing on without giving up?

Then why did she do it? Why did she
jump into the deep well?

Because she just wanted to stop all
her pain; stop it once for all.

When she cannot tear out even a single page of
her life, she threw the whole book in the fire."

Killing one self was, anyway, a misnomer. She didn't attempt to kill herself. She thought that she was simply defeated by the long, hard struggle to stay alive. You may agree that she truly fought so hard.

Many times we are inclined to that in a suicide no fight was involved, and that somebody simply gave up. This was quite wrong in most of the cases. On the other end,

"When people kill themselves, they think
they're ending the pain, but all they're doing is
passing it on to those they leave behind."
- Jeannette Walls

Here, Amsaveni had left behind her son, who was fifteen months old and was sleeping peacefully in the cradle, hoping to see his mother when he wakes up. In a matter of fifteen months from his birth, all had come to an end; the mother was no more there, and now what will be the little boys' future? At least in the case of Amsaveni and Alwarappan, they had been taken care of, educated and given basic needs to face the world, but this fifteen month baby which had survived among all other four conceptions and had also battled all the nine months journey in his mother's womb and had coped up with the ever changing family atmosphere of his father and mother throughout his life had now come to a standstill situation due to his mother's decision. Father was still unwilling to take up the family responsibility or that of his son but ran away from all of it once for all.

CHAPTER 6

IT'S NOT OVER YET

Amsaveni thought she was dead, including her many thought it all ended here. She felt that she had finally succeeded. She felt for a moment that when she jumped into the well, all her problems would come to an end. She said to herself, 'at moment of death, all my troubles seemed to go far away forever. I am out of the clutches of my managers, out of any trouble from the society, out of every problem caused by my husband, yes I miss my son, but I'm sure he'll be in good hands.

This is the day all my pains and struggles will finally cease. No. She heard something else; she could hear voices which were disturbing and very much human. The sounds were feeble and very mild. Her senses were active, she felt very much alive. She felt agonizing pain in certain areas and numbness in the other parts of her body. She definitely felt being carried somewhere…

Hold her, put the body on the right side,
don't stand and cry over here, She is not yet
dead; there are still signs of life, Move!
Move! Don't stand in the way!

She couldn't believe that she was hearing these voices, as if she was alive. She could hear the distant voice of her mother and her sisters. She was still thinking how they could have known that she jumped in the well. "How is it possible that I'm hearing their cries? Is it my funeral, am I not fully dead? Is it possible that dead people can hear others? The more she thought, the more prominent were the voices.

She's started hearing voices, "Amsaveni, why did you do this? Why such a decision? Didn't you think of us? Didn't you think of your little boy?" The louder the sound came, the more she started feeling alive. She tried opening her eyes but she couldn't as the severity of the pain was increasing. She could hear the hospital noises and some patients crying in pain. For a moment, she had recollected the thought of having climbed on a rope tied ladder from the well, and falling back again. She fostered the thought of wanting to just go back a few hours, recollect from her memory and wanting to confirm for sure that she was dead and no more alive.

With a little difficulty, she started recollecting the events in the last few hours. Now she could see that she was at the point where she was standing in the edge and trying to jump into the well. For the last time she remembered that she had gathered all her strength and had jumped. She heard the sound of the water splashing. She could remember that the water was so cold and the well's deep silence and pitch darkness had increased her fear and anxiety.

Though for a moment she felt relieved, the fear that crept in made her scream. She could hear herself screaming as loud as possible from a depth of one hundred meters inside the well. The more she screamed, the more her fear increased. She could hear some voices from the top asking, "Who is this? What happened? She's the daughter of the teacher Sundaram Pillai and she jumped into the well." She continued to cry for help.

It was still half past four in the morning. The news spread like wild fire. People started gathering all around the well. News had spread to her home. They couldn't believe that it was Amsaveni; they went inside her room and confirmed that she wasn't there.

By this time, she could see a ladder coming down the well and many voices shouting "Climb up and come" "Hold the ladder" etc. She was confident of holding the ladder and she started climbing. She was just happy to be out of the fear of darkness. The ladder was pulled amidst many screaming voices and disturbances. The ladder was oscillating with her body hitting against the stones, and scratching against the walls. She held on tight. In that moment with too many people holding and pulling the ladder, she knew that she was going to be out. But as the well was used for drinking, they had a pulley fixed in that corner which was protruding the entrance of the well. People were more careless when holding the ladder. They were not trained professionals to rescue somebody from emergency situations like this. They are only trying their best.

Alas! So unfortunate that before they could pull the ladder up, the ladder mistakenly got hit with the pulley with such force and Amsaveni missed the grip on the ladder and was thrown back inside. Since it wasn't a straight fall, she hit her back against a strong stone on the wall and became unconscious. Completely unconscious, she fell back into the waters. This time she knew nothing; she was drowning. Her brother had gone already to call the fire station and was waiting for them to come. By the time he reached the spot, all these things took place. The fire station came only to pick up the unconscious body that was drowning.

She remembered only this - She had screamed on the hospital bed, realizing that she was not dead. She was hit even harder, "an accident inside a suicide". What a tragedy to comprehend! Misfortune never comes alone, but was ruling her life, one after another. All that she thought had come to an end had not. Death had still not accepted her plea; it was dragging her on every bit. The soul which did not belong to her couldn't accept her choice of killing it in suicide. She doesn't have the authority over her soul and spirit. Death denied her to do such an evil thing, to end her life in such a way and spend eternity in hell.

But the human mind cannot fathom the purpose the Creator has for each of His creation. Without a purpose, nothing is created in this universe. Every living and non-living thing has a purpose. Amsaveni came to the conclusion of ending her life, she decided everything and was destined to ruin. She wanted to proceed no more. But the purpose for which she has been created had not been completed; even death denied her entry to the next world, unless she fulfilled her responsibility.

At great tough periods, many of us have always felt deep within us the temptation to commit suicide. We yielded ourselves to it, breached our own defenses. The idea of suicide is a protest against life; by dying, maybe we think we would escape this longing for death, but we do not have the right to end the life which was not created by us.

Here she was on the hospital bed, groaning in pain and agony, tears continuously rolling down her eyes. Down from her neck, she could only feel a burning pain and inexpressible discomfort. She also couldn't feel her hand, leg or any other part of her body. Her T4 lumbar region spinal cord had been crushed in her second fall. The nerve that goes to the lower part of the body from the hip down had completely crushed (but not cut).

Her whole family from her mother's side was standing there, weeping and questioning her. She couldn't answer anymore, she didn't want to answer. She wanted to end everything but here she was again in an utterly helpless situation.

Anyone who has been close to someone that has attempted suicide knows, there is no other pain like that felt after the incident, and especially at the given situation for Amsaveni, words are not enough to describe.

Fast forwarding from February 1986, for the next year and a half, the tragedy in hospital was more heartbreaking than all the troubles put together so far. At first, on the day of the incident, she was brought to the Government hospital in her locality, and since it was a suicide attempt case which calls for Police involvement, it had to be treated only in a Government hospital. Even so, her family was not in any position or mindset to move her to a private hospital. Moreover in those days, not many private hospitals were equipped to handle such cases unless it was in Chennai, the capital city.

The Government hospital didn't have all the professional equipment or support to handle her situation; nevertheless they were treating her for more than a year with her broken back. They couldn't perform any operation on her broken spinal cord as her back had developed a "deep bed sore". (Bed sores, also known as pressure ulcers are skin lesions which can be caused by friction, humidity, high temperature and unrelieved pressure. Any part of the body may be affected. If discovered early they can be treated, but most of the time at the later stage they are fatal).

To explain the situation of the bed sore in a few lines, not going into detail - The back part of the body from the lung bone until the tail bone just above the buttock muscle, was gradually eaten by the bed sore germs. At one point it came to a situation where a full bottle of honey was poured inside and the bones were very much visible to the naked eyes. Her mother couldn't bear to witness what was happening to her daughter.

Was it the carelessness of the Hospital medical attendants or was it Amsaveni's fate? What shall we call it? At the age of 27, a young woman was in a situation which no one would dare to dream would happen.

When they came to a point where the bed sore started producing germs, the doctors washed off their hands and had told to take her to Chennai Stanley Hospital as they couldn't handle the situation furthermore. Who will take her to Chennai?

Who will give the required financial, physical and moral support?

Already each of her family members was going through their own measures of trials and tough times. Adding to that, for the past one year, they were supporting her medical situation as well.

Meanwhile, her husband who was initially at the hospital for the first few days had eloped. Yes, he was afraid of the police case and rejection from his and Amsaveni's families. Neither could he face any questions, nor was he willing to take up the responsibility of his dying wife and his infant in the cradle.

In the first few weeks, Amsaveni needed a bottle of blood and fortunately both Alwarappan's and Amsaveni's blood was A+. He agreed to give a bottle of blood to his wife soon after the accident. After that, he absconded; he locked the house where they both lived, kept the key in an envelope sent it to Amsaveni's mother by post and vanished. From that day onwards for nearly four years, Amsaveni or her family did not know any whereabouts of him. Gradually even his own family did not know where he was.

Coming back to her medical situation being transferred to Chennai, her brother and her elder sister (who earlier settled in Chennai) volunteered, her younger sisters were asked to help, and with the effort of the other family members, she was now in Stanley Medical Hospital Chennai. All were hoping that somehow they could see their sister walking again and getting back to her normal life. Now from all sides, people were comforting her. Her mother dedicated all her time to Amsaveni. Shifting to the hospital in Chennai had not made any progressive improvement on her health.

The bed sores on her back were rotting from inside out, penetrating deeper and deeper every day.

What kind of a situation was Amsaveni in?
Self-pity?
Is Self-pity a sin?
Is it a form of living suicide?

Now where was the little infant? Before his mother's attempt to commit suicide, he was in the cradle, a little boy of one year and three months. Now where could he be without his father and mother?

Left all alone?

Suicide doesn't end the pain. It just gives it to someone else.

Has it been given to him?

What moments or days can Amsaveni remember or would like to remember at this situation?

We do not remember the days, we remember the moments. The richness of one's life lies in forgotten memories.

You have a choice - Live or die. Every breath is a choice. Every minute is a choice. To be or not to be. But you should have a purpose to pursue, which will motivate you, direct you, and makes each of your steps meaningful. What was lacking – a drive, a consistent desire to live, a pursuit of excellence?

Life is only a long and bitter suicide, and faith alone can transform this suicide into sacrifice. Was it possible?

On a daily course of pain and agony with no improvement from any treatment, at one point the doctors came to a conclusion. As the medicines were not working in her body and since her bedsores were eating up all her flesh, there was no strength in her body and in her spirit to pull on anymore. The only best suggestion they could give was "let's suggest mercy killing, but we need legal permission". They thought that at least it would free her from this life of trauma and pain which was unexplainable. At this young age of 27, she has gone through enough and more in her body and in her mind. What's left for her to hold on to?

Even at one point, one of the attendants had commented to Amsaveni's mother – "you better throw her in the ocean and walk away, it's not worth living like this". Amsaveni wasn't aware that she was being prepared for the second killing, instead of getting killed by the bedsore worms, sleepless nights for years together, no sensations from neck to toe, groaning pain all over her spine (it's still not recovered from the crushed nerve damage), wasn't it better to end it once for all again?

No words to console and no options to comprehend further. The lightning grief had struck the whole family. No ray of hope from any corner of the world, nor from any man, not from any beliefs or the fasts she had for many idols. But none could comprehend that it was a just the beginning of a new chapter in her life. The path to a unique experience, the path to the IMPACT, towards the one experience that's going to excel in her life time, it's not the end, it has only begun.

Who will educate her little boy?

Where will her little boy live?

Who will provide him food and shelter?

What happened to Alwarappan? Did they meet ever again?

Could they ever live together again?

Was she killed in the hospital due to failure of treatment? Did they threw her at the ocean?

Is there any hope to recover? Is there any possibility to think of life again?

What good can come out of her again?

Hopeless?   Clueless?   Unacceptable?   Unbearable? Unbelievable?

Any other words to describe her current situation? Who can help her now?

Is there a solution? Is there an answer to all these questions?

CHAPTER 7

AMSAVENI IS NOW 54

It's Feb 4, 2013. Amsaveni was feeling breathless from morning. She thought it's due to the climate in Bangalore city, India. She felt she'll be alright in some time, she held on till the evening but with difficulty. Alwarappan was asking her, if he has to call anybody for help. She said, let me call my son and ask him.

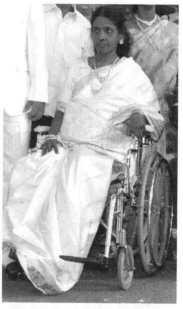

She then made a call to her son who was in Abu Dhabi, United Arab Emirates at 6 pm (Indian Time). Amsaveni called her son and said she's feeling breathless from morning, and asked him what to do? Her son mentioned that when they spoke the previous day, she sounded fine. Amsaveni responded saying, it's just the climate and she should be fine soon. This is her first experience with breathlessness, and as its increasing she doesn't know what to do. Her son responded saying, "not to worry mom, I will tell my friends now, someone will come now, and take you in Ambulance to hospital. If you want me to come; I'll book a flight and will come in few days".

Amsaveni told her son not to come, as she can manage by herself. She just told she needs some help, and hence asked him to send his friends. She also pointed out that he had just come before three months ago for their new house dedication and her granddaughter's naming ceremony. She was concerned that he needs to take leave again and spend for flight again. She said she can manage as it's not very serious.

Son, made a few calls to his friends and also to his sister in law, who lives at a distance from her mother's home and updated the situation. They called the Ambulance and arranged to pick Amsaveni to hospital.

Though her son had arranged the needful, he felt very disturbed with her tone in the phone. Had called up his friend, who is a travel agent to check if there was any flight available to Bangalore that night or in that week. He reached home from his office, and discussed with his wife, about the call from his mom. She comforted him and told will pray for Amsaveni and she will be fine soon. He was still feeling restless. He called up few of his well-wishers and each one was comforting him. The reason for the breathlessness could have been the climate.

His heart was not at peace. His spirit was restless. He was anxious to meet his mom and decided to go immediately. He called up his friend again on the ticket availability. His friend said there was no flight available from Abu Dhabi to Bangalore for next three days and that international flights couldn't be booked at the last minute. He assured him that he would try to book the next available flight three days later.

After hanging up, he was still anxious. So he told his wife that he would be going to Bangalore that day and was looking if any flight was available. While he was still packing, he was praying that somehow he wanted to see his mom, as her voice was not that alright and he felt she was in pain.

Suddenly he stopped and thought what if his mom wanted to meet his wife and daughter when he is going to meet her? Though they had just come from India, three months back, still this thought was lingering in his mind. He then told his wife to pack her bags to go to Bangalore. She immediately cooperated with him and packed the needful for their trip.

By now, it's already 8pm in Abu Dhabi, and the last flight from Abu Dhabi to Bangalore is about to be departed in 2 hours' time, which means by now they should have checked-in. He called his friend and said that he wanted to leave that night to Bangalore and to book a flight for him and his family in any possible way. His friend said that it was impossible to get one ticket at this last minute, forget about getting a family ticket. But the son was insisting to book any available ticket. Some of his well-wishers reached home and were encouraging him, and with a short word of prayer, the son, his wife and his daughter started to travel towards the airport without even having a ticket in hand. The son was praying that he will definitely get a ticket as he was really looking forward to meet his mom.

His friend called up now and said you really have a great favor from above; a miracle took place. Last minute, one family had missed the flight and his friend (travel agent) got those three tickets in hand, however it was to Mumbai (which is 2 hour flight journey from Bangalore, Amsaveni's place). He would have to catch the flight in the next ten minutes. As his son had already started and was on the way by faith, he reached the airport within next ten minutes and as a family they were heading towards Mumbai. All this happened in a matter of three hours from the time Amsaveni called.

From Mumbai Airport to Bangalore airport, domestic ticket needs to be taken. It's already midnight in India. His wife said she'll try to book that ticket by asking her friend. She tried calling her friend and in-spite of the late hours, her friend picked up the call, understood the emergency and told she'll get back to her shortly. But as the air hostess was telling everyone to switch off the mobile due to flight take off, without any option the phone was switched off. Now that they are on the flight they were not sure if they will have a ticket to Bangalore when they landed in Mumbai airport. His 8-month old daughter was very calm, in-spite of the sudden travel. Meanwhile, his wife's friend booked an online ticket and had messaged the booking reference to her while they were still on flight.

As soon they landed in Mumbai Airport, they received the booking reference just in time. The desire to meet Amsaveni was growing in both of their hearts, but all these unexpected but yet unbelievable flight tickets are getting booked on time, they both could feel a supernatural favour and grace from above. He then remembered his mom's quote from the Book she used to read every day.

"May he give you the desire of your heart and make all your plans succeed" and "Commit your ways unto Him, trust also in Him and He will do it"

From Mumbai, after having an hour of stop over, from International terminal to Domestic terminal then to the check-in, now the son and his wife with their daughter were now heading towards Bangalore airport.

Meanwhile, Amsaveni who had been taken in an Ambulance was not being admitted to the nearby hospital. Her condition was getting critical and doctor's suggested to get admitted in ICU immediately but there was no bed available in that hospital, moving from one hospital to another, she was finally admitted.

By now her son with his wife and daughter landed in Bangalore airport and reached directly to the hospital around 10.30 am the following day (Feb 5, 2013).

He enquired the status of Amsaveni and his friends who were there waiting for him, updated that her condition was very critical last night and right now she was in ICU under observation.

The doctors have not come back yet to meet her. So far, only blood samples were taken from Amsaveni. The son was allowed inside the ICU to meet his mom.

Fighting though the pain, but with an ever smiling face, she looked up and saw her son approaching her. That was an emotional moment for both mother and son. She stretched forth her hand and signaled her son to come near. She stretched forth towards his son and pulled him towards her bosom and gave a tight hug like never before. This was the first time he ever experienced a hug like that from his mom.

As she was hugging, she was whispering in her son's ears, that she was going through a difficult time for few hours last night and was almost about to die. She prayed that only after meeting her son she will close her eyes forever. She said she was very much sure that he will come to see her and her faith was proven once again. That one hug which is indescribable lasted for few amazing moments.

Just as the son expected, Amsaveni asked for her daughter in-law and granddaughter. Her son in his spirit knew it, and with happy yet taxing emotions, he said that they are here with him. He went out and let his wife go in and meet her inside the Intensive Care Unit (ICU). Her son showed her granddaughter over the glass door, being an infant her little granddaughter was not permitted inside the ICU. Amsaveni spoke to her daughter in law for some time.

Alwarappan was standing out there and was explaining the events of the previous day to his son. As the daughter in law came out, the son went again to see his mom. Now Amsaveni had asked him to bring for her fruit juice to drink and food to eat. With the doctor's permission, the son had brought in the food and juice and Amsaveni had asked him to feed her. With mixed emotions, the son was sitting next to his mother and was feeding her as he fed her for last two decades.

Though she couldn't eat all of it, she did have her heart full. Now the doctor had come with the blood results and had told, it's just urinary infection. They were waiting for few more results on urine culture test and they suspect there may be a possibility of Urosepsis (urinary infection entering the blood stream). But assured that her condition is normal as of now and she will be alright in next few days.

In between the conversations, the doctor was more curious and asked Amsaveni's son, as to how it was possible to keep her alive for twenty seven long years in bed ridden condition. It is medically impossible, with the condition she was in. He brought in few more doctors and with a perplexed expression he was explaining that it was nearly impossible to maintain a paraplegic person for twenty seven long years. Her son was giving the details of her life and was telling her testimony of strength and courage, her inspiration and the secret of living her bed ridden life to the doctors and was praising the goodness of the Creator and the mercy and favour HE had showered on her all these years.

While he was still speaking, he kept an eye on his mom's face and noticed that she wanted to tell him something. He excused himself and went near to his mom, and she began to speak saying: Son, I will be happy even if I die now. I'm the happiest woman. If I would've died before 27 years when I jumped into the well, I would have reached hell and would've spent rest of my life in eternal damnation. But now, I'm so happy and content that we had lived as a family. I saw you earning degrees and had secured a good name in society and placed in a good position abroad. Though I miss some days of staying with you lately, still I understand that you have to grow up in your life and I will never be a stumbling block in your career. She said, as she read in the

Book so it happened to her, ("HE gives strength to the weary and gives power to the weak")

She said all the later part of her life, she sustained herself in the living words of that Book, every situation she was in, every time she needs help, she used to get back to that Book and she will be comforted. She referred to one of her favourite lines of the Book and quoted.

"Though the mountains be shaken and the hills be removed, yet my unfailing love for you will not be shaken nor my covenant of peace be removed,".

Yes He has been faithful in what HE said.

"Faithful is HE who had called me, and had sustained me until this end".

She continued to talk, "I'm so happy that you got married to the girl whom I chose for you. She will take care of you from now on. She is the wise woman as mentioned in that Book.

I'm more joyous to be a grandmother. I also feel so happy to have played with my grandchild (Fiammetta) during the last four months and dedicate her for His glory. I have also seen and blessed your first property. I would have missed all this wonderful moments, if I had passed away when I had jumped in to the well, 27 years before or in the severity of bed sore. But now, tell me what more I can ask of my creator.

She referred to her beloved Book, which she always refer to her son, saying, "it is good that I have been afflicted, so that I had learnt His ways, I had experienced His love and

I have cherished His relationship all these years which He added to my life.

She still continued to talk and told him to bring his daughter up in a morally and spiritually disciplined way and should teach about the Book that had changed her life, her son's life and her husband's life. She said to her son, to take care of her husband, his father as he'll be left alone after her departure.

By now, the doctor was asking him to leave the place as she's in ICU and needs rest. So he left the hospital, went home freshened up and came back to see Amsaveni again. He came back to the ICU ward and asked for permission to meet Amsaveni again.

At the same time, Amsaveni, requested the doctor as she wanted to talk to her son. The doctor cautioned her son to leave once he finished talking and left the place. Amsaveni asked her son to pray for her, and told him to lay hand on her head and pray. With unexplainable emotions, the son laid his one hand on her head and in the other hand he was holding her hand and was praying.

After a minute or so, the son opened his eyes to see his mom and the next second she opened her eyes, looked straight into his eyes and just closed her eyes once for all. Two drops of tears rolled down her cheeks.

This is it. She breathed her last! A peaceful entry to her eternal life, a glorious ending of her earthly life!!!

Wow! What a glorious ending. Just a heart-warming experience to her son, who felt so privileged and honoured to be there and experience the final moments of his mother's life.

Amsaveni's son believed firmly that his mom would have uttered the similar words which he read in that Book.

"Sovereign father, as you have promised, you
may now dismiss your servant in peace.
For my eyes have seen your salvation, which you
have prepared in the sight of all nations"
"Precious in the sight of the Creator,
is the death of His saints."

In-spite of all odds, she stood as a witness for what she read in that Book,

"I have fought the good fight, I have finished
the race, I have kept the faith"

Being miles away yet her son had made it to reach her and the last few precious hours she spent with her son, she spoke her heart out. Her son prayed for her and she departed to a better place. All her physical pain came to a rest and her spirit went to the One who has created it. What a blessed ending to Amsaveni's life, a complete life in itself.

Rewinding back twenty seven years, the first attempt of Amsaveni to end her life, which she had thought will end it all and comparing that with the end which she just had twenty seven years later, so remarkable and so peaceful, which one would long for.

So, what was the change agent?

What had happened to her in these years?

How was she able to sit, move and respond?

What had happened to her in these years?

Can such things happen to a woman who had lost everything and was utterly hopeless and was facing death to have such an honorable and glorious ending?

Can she make such honest confessions of her happiness and contentment?

Was it all a dream? Is this possible?

Who gave her answers to her past miseries? Who delivered her from her helpless situation?

How it all happened?

How and when did Alwarappan come back and live with Amsaveni?

How her little boy she left before had grown up and being part of this glorious ending?

CHAPTER 8

AMSAVENI'S LITTLE BOY

Amsaveni joy knew no bounds as she saw her son grew into a man who cared for her for all these years, and was now a father to her granddaughter. Her life had fully revolved around her son for more than two decades now. This was the boy whom she prayed for, whom she conceived after two abortions and whose birth had saved her marriage and family. This was the boy whom she considered to be the best gift in all her uncertainties, and who was privileged to be with his mother until she breathed her last.

OK, then why did she leave him and attempt suicide?

Didn't she feel for her son then?

Yes, she did think about him. However, with trials and troubles thrown at her from all sides, she was forced to take that step. But the rest of her life was focused on the Book and her son alone. The Book, which made her alive once again, which gave her the inner peace and confidence which she didn't have before and which gave her the desire to live for others, was kept close

to her heart She believed that the Book had enabled her to bring her son and her family up to this stage, from all impossibilities that resulted from a bed ridden life.

Her son whom she saw as a baby, as an abandoned child of fifteen months, was now a man, who had a job, was married and now a father himself; yet he was still a little boy to Amsaveni.

She still vividly remembered the day her son came to meet her in the hospital when he was only 4 years old. She was on the bed, looking up with no sensation whatsoever, from her neck to her toes. She was only able to speak and turn her head from side to side. When she saw her little boy approaching her, she saw the little infant whom she left in cradle on February 1986 when he was just 1 year and 3 months, who was now walking up to her after 3 years. She couldn't raise her hands and hug him. She couldn't lift him and cuddle him. She could not feed him nor ask him anything. Just tears rolled down her cheeks, tears of love, pain, helplessness; tears that words couldn't explain. By this time, the operation on her spinal cord was successful. She was now able to turn and lie on her back. This was the best that had happened to her in three years since she believed the Book without even knowing that it was meant for her. She didn't give her fullest attention to that Book, yet she believed that just because of that one Book which she had read, had changed her helpless body to gain strength and had equipped her internal strength to endure her first operation on her back.

The little boy who was standing next to her asked her many questions, but didn't get any response. He spent the next few hours with her running between the beds, taking the fruits and items on the table next to his mother, and playing with it. Amsaveni remembered all the troubles she went through during her 9 month pregnancy to bring this baby boy out into this world.

She wanted to live again. She wanted to rise up, sit, stand and walk again. She wanted to run to her little boy, and hug him and kiss him. She wanted to take care of him and face life again for his sake. She felt she could do it; though her body was dead and had no sense, yet her spirit was willing to do it. She didn't know how or whether it was even possible. But yes, she had the desire to do it.

It worked!!! For yet another year, she was in the hospital, going through treatment for her back; she was trying her best to regain control of her senses, mainly she was attempting to get her renal functions under control. This miracle didn't happen in a day or two, but slowly and steadily took a whole year. She gained her senses little by little, and step by step she was gaining grounds. She could soon sense her neck, then her shoulders, then her hands, her stomach and then her hips. It is the most challenging part of her life; but she had hope, she had the will power to regain her stability, and she wanted to face this world once again for her son. She couldn't bear the image of her son looking at her, so helpless and hopeless.

On the other side, she often cried bitterly that she couldn't walk; she, who had walked for 27 years, could no longer walk.

She was bed-ridden for the rest of her life. Even if she wants to drink a glass of water, she had to ask someone to help her. Even if she was hungry, unless someone comes to her and gives her food, she couldn't eat. What a pathetic situation? For everything she had to depend on somebody. This dependency was killing her. The insults and criticism of the people around her didn't spare her either.

Now in all this, she comforted herself that;

"All things happen for good, to those who believe in Him"

She overcame her struggles in the hospital, and was finally discharged after four long years there. Now her son was five years old. He was sometimes taken care of by Amsaveni sisters, and sometimes left alone to take care of himself. Though her little boy was the only male heir of her husband's family (among his five brothers and one sister), still no one had come to see him, or took care of him. His father who ran away during the first month when Amsaveni was in the hospital had still not returned.

None of the family members knew whether he was dead or alive, no one knew his whereabouts. But here is Amsaveni, with a limited support from her mother's family but yet with a strong will power to face the renewed life she received from the Book.

Now that five year old boy was made her first nurse at home; the attendant to take care of his ailing mother on bed. From helping her in brushing her teeth, from helping her to do her morning routine to bathing, he was the only attendant for her. Amsaveni's brother was kind enough to keep her in his home; her sisters helped in all possible ways; her parents were happy that their daughter is alive, but couldn't bear to see her bed ridden state for the rest of her life.

Just a few weeks after her return, she happened to meet her sister's friends from the school where her sister worked as a teacher. Three of them, Sheila Daniel, Hannah Benjamin and Suriya Benjamin who came to see her, were filled with a burden to pray for her life after they heard her story. They wanted to lead her to the knowledge of the Book she was referring to.

It was not easy for Amsaveni to leave all her old traditions and beliefs, and do something totally new or meaningful at once. It took time for her to battle between her past beliefs and present. It raised so many questions of fear, guilt and confusion.

Amsaveni was convinced that the Book which she was reading gave her life back; the Book had restored her broken life. The words of the Book gave her hope and an indescribable internal peace which she was longing for all these years. But her old traditions, habits, and beliefs which were a part of her for all these years, couldn't come to an end so easily.

Now that she was living at her brother's home with a large family of her unmarried sisters, parents, it was not easy for her to seek clarification of the change inside her. She couldn't ask anyone about that Book which speaks of true life. She couldn't ask clarifications or reasonable explanations about the creation of the human kin d, their purpose in this earth, the reason of this current world's pathetic state, the hope to endure future.

Here stood three women who came through a divine appointment, met her at her home, next to her bed, determined to pray for her life and explain all her queries one by one.

They showed compassion on her son, they wanted him to be educated, they wanted him to grow up in the knowledge of the Book, which his mother wanted to understand, which has brought back his mother to life again.

(from left) Krishnaveni (Amsaveni's sister), Surya Benjamin, Sheela Daniel and Hannah Benjamin

Along with these three women, there was one more woman named Ruby who lived two buildings away from Amsaveni's brother's home. As soon as she came to know about her, she came to meet her. She extended her time and support to Amsaveni to call her whenever she wanted to ask any questions regarding that Book. She also advised Amsaveni to make her little boy read the Book and memorize it every day. She left a deep impact on Amsaveni with her statement, "make your son read and carry this Book at this age, and this Book will carry him for the rest of his life" which penetrated Amsaveni's heart.

The three friends of her sister and this fourth woman had become strong pillars of support in helping Amsaveni understand the Book in a better way. She still wasn't completely convinced. She believed there is truth, she believed there is life, she believed there is hope; but in her current situation, she couldn't practice what she was reading. This didn't stop her from encouraging her little boy in reading the Book. Every day morning, she would make sure he memorized at least five lines from the Book. The way she would make him do this was interesting. Every day when he woke up, after helping his mother in brushing her teeth and doing the morning chores, he had to prepare tea or coffee. Before he drank, she would ask him to memorize 5 lines and say it aloud before touching the tea cup. This practice was not only in the morning, but repeated at night before eating dinner. She would ask him to recite the lines he had memorized the previous day and the current day together. It was the most stressful and hateful process the little boy was going through. But it turned out to be fruitful for the rest of his life. Though Amsaveni's son didn't like the way his mother was making him read the Book, he continued to do it due to her loving compulsion.

Her son was her motivation to live again. The situations she had to go through in order to provide education and clothing to him were heartbreaking. Amsaveni's brother had a son who was as old as her son; they both lived in the same home, and they were more like twins in the house. But the conditions of their upbringing were completely different; the comfort which both the boys received was different. Her little boy would cry to Amsaveni asking her to buy him good clothes, pencils, school bag etc., she could not respond to the little boy's needs apart from giving him a hug and telling him that she would get it soon.

Only she knew that the word 'soon' would never be possible in the near future. She was no longer in a position to work again; her husband was not there with them anymore and she was living at the mercy of her brother and parent's family. Her heart was willing to get up, work and earn money to meet her son's needs. But physically it was not possible. Though she wanted to do it all, she still needed support to sit, move, go out of the home, etc.

She finally started working again!!! She did it with the hope gained everyday by the comforting words she received from that Book, and the four women who were determined to pray for her life. She made a choice to take tuitions for the children around her home, by lying in the bed. She had her son help her get ready, sit with support and spend three hours in the evening to teach the school children, by which she can earn some money for her little boy. It was a herculean task for both Amsaveni and her son to do this every single day, but Amsaveni wanted to take care of him, and to provide him with her hard earned money. She didn't want to ask anyone, she didn't want to live on the sympathy of any one, she didn't want wanted to blame her situation and do nothing about it, She based her decision on the words of the Book; she based her motivation on her little boy's life, and she did it.

She undertook the task of tutoring the children around her home, until her son completed education. She felt that she should continue to do it even though it was little money. Though her son started earning and supporting her, still that little amount she earned made her feel good.

In contrast, Alwarappan who had a good beginning and the most comfortable life at his father's home, after the marriage and until Amsaveni's death at the age of 54, could never hold on to a permanent job, hence was unable to provide financial stability to his family. He stubbornly continued living in his ego, unable to work for anyone due to his temper and sharp tongue. Yet in all of this, he never got himself in any bad habits of drinking, smoking or anything of that sort.

He was innocent in his own way. Yet, when the words of that Book which gave life to Amsaveni had met Alwarappan in a unique way, he became a changed person and was a tremendous support to Amsaveni in the final ten years of her life. You will read more about him in the coming chapters.

Now Amsaveni and her son started to attract the attention of Amsaveni's father and family members due to her profound change, by reading that Book and also the difference in her habitual beliefs. Amsaveni had a very strong reason on how she finally came to the decision that the one person mentioned in that Book is her soul winner and Saviour. But her words of explanation did not help her family members to comprehend her belief or conviction, rather it resulted in persecution and monitoring. Even further the change in Amsaveni's beliefs was considered a shame and an insult to their community and beliefs.

There had been times when both Amsaveni and her little boy would read that Book when everyone slept, in the night lamp where no one could notice them. Ruby, their neighbor, would take Amsaveni's little boy on Sundays to teach him more about that Book and its importance. At one point even she was prohibited from stepping into the house by Amsaveni's parents.

Even the three women Sheila, Hena and Suriya who occasionally came to meet Amsaveni to pray with her and speak on the Book, they were scorned by her family members.

The words of the Book which brought her out of the claws of death, which encouraged her to look at life in a different way with more meaning to it, which sustained her in her bed ridden condition, which enabled her to regain her senses up to the hip and start working again for her little boy, which had brought these four women in the most appropriate time of her life, had caused her to bring her out of her parent's home in the most miraculous way and paved her a new channel of support and understanding.

Amsaveni's boy who had seen from the time he could remember, his mother in a bed ridden condition until the day of her death, and had seen his father for the first time when he was six and was introduced to him just like a stranger, and who had seen criticism, pain, shame, embarrassment and scorn under societal pressure and from his peer group could not comprehend as to why all this had to happen to him alone.

He questioned,

"Why me? Why are all dark days only for me?"

This boy during his teen years felt the peer pressure and had to face the temptations of this world just like any other boy of his age. He couldn't find realistic hope inside his family. He always saw his mother on bed and father without a job. He did the best he could while listening to his mother and doing all the needful - from taking care of his mother, to doing all the house chores, working in petty jobs and being responsible in his studies. He felt that his life had no meaning apart from slogging.

He felt loneliness, lack of love and care, and had to struggle every day to have three meals food. There have been days he went continuously for more than a week without food. Just like his mother, he reached a point of taking out his own life and consistently attempted different methods of suicide. Four times he failed.

The fifth time, he went up a mountain top with a decision to jump. He didn't have anyone to share his emotional pain, but the Creator had a definite purpose for him. He didn't realize it at that age. He was very close to jumping, he heard a voice. A voice that shook his life, a Voice that so lovingly called him by his name. Amsaveni didn't know any of this, she earnestly prayed for her son. Her prayer saved him; her son had a unique experience with his Creator. From that day onwards, during the next month his heart searched for the reason behind that Voice.

He obeyed to that Voice on 26 February 2000. Amsaveni was so glad that her son chose to follow his Creator from his heart. From that day onwards, her son had seen so much of positive energy within him. He also found favor in the eyes of men. All the works of his hands were blessed. The next month was his board exam; ended up being the top rank holder, and soon afterwards pursued his higher studies with scholarship.

Amsaveni believed in bringing up her son by following the instructions from the Book. As she couldn't be with him all the time nor could monitor him every minute, she felt that her teachings would definitely help him in his future days. She would often quote some of the below lines from that Book,

"Train up a child, in the way he should go, so
that when he is old, he'll not depart from it"

"Discipline your son, and he will give you
rest; he will give delight to your heart"

"The rod and reproof give wisdom, but a child
left to him brings shame to his mother"

Many times, she had told her personal life story to her son. His mother was his only friend for many years. She spoke to him on all the areas of her life, and used to tell him that whatever you do and behave outside home, speaks about her and about her upbringing inside home.

She would tell him about his birth and things related to that, and encourage him with the words from the Book,

"For He formed your inward parts; he knitted you together
in your mother's womb. So praise him, for you are
fearfully and wonderfully made. Wonderful are his works"

"Before you are formed in my womb He knew you,
and before you were born He consecrated you."

Amsaveni's son was very mischievous when he grew up. It was not easy for Amsaveni to discipline him so easily. She used to fast and pray for him every day, and counsel him with these words from the Book.

"Honor your father and mother so that it may go well with you, and that you may enjoy long life on earth."

"Listen my son, to your father's instruction and do not forsake your mother's teaching. They will be a garland to grace your head and a chain to adorn your neck".

"Do not withhold discipline from a child; if you strike him with a rod, he will not die. If you strike him with the rod, you will save his soul from destruction"

All the words of wisdom with gentle correction truly helped Amsaveni's son to align his life at every stage. He also found favour in the eyes of his mother's and father's families, and they came forward to help him as much as they could in bringing the family together.

Those words in the Book helped the little boy to grow up in wisdom and understanding; those words which had encouraged his mother had encouraged him, in the days of loneliness, in the days of denied food and clothing. Those words of the Book were the only support and surviving kit for the boy during the teenage temptations. All those words his mother made him memorize had helped him during moments of despair, loneliness, insecurity and fear when the boy reached his teens.

After his schooling, he continued his college studies, and after earning his Masters' degree, he started to work in an IT firm in Bangalore. Shortly afterwards, he moved abroad and is now working in Abu Dhabi.

CHAPTER 9

A MOTHER-IN-LAW AND
A GRANDMOTHER

"**If there should be a change, let me be the change, and let the change start from me.** In my son's marriage, there should not be any dowry, there should not be disparity, there should not be indifference, and there should not be any demand from bridegroom side to bride side"

Marriage is the first institution established by the Creator, a holy and divinely established covenant. It's not the "ceremony" that is important in a marriage, it is the couple's covenant and commitment before the Creator and the witnesses. The bride and Bridegroom are equal in this marriage partnership. Both of them have their own credits, which they bring to this long lasting relationship. Be it finance, rituals, wedding arrangements and other responsibilities, all have to be shared between the families.

Many of Amsaveni's well-wishers criticized her on this matter. They said that she didn't know the world, she didn't know how to make use of this opportunity; by being the mother to a son who is earning well and settled abroad, she was missing the chance to demand good dowry. Amsaveni's response to all of their criticism was never justification nor arguments, but a mere "silence".

On a different note, she told them that she was looking for a woman of wisdom and prayer, who could stand with him at all times and build a loving family with her son; the marriage had to be based on love, truth and transparency and never on money. It's not we who are going to live inside their marriage partnership, it's the couple and it's their relationship in understanding each other and building a strong interpersonal relationship between them, keeping the Creator in their midst.

She very firmly used to say, as mentioned in the Book,

"What the Creator has united let no man, money, materialism, rituals, or nothing separate"

Amsaveni and Alwarappan started praying for their son's marriage who had just left for United Arab Emirates. As a regular practice, her church pastor gave a list of boys and girls who are ready for marriage to all the elderly couples to pray for them. As they were praying for some days, one morning as usual Amsaveni prayed for each name on the list; she came to the name "Roshni" and stopped for a moment. She asked Alwarappan, "Have we seen this girl? I don't remember. Do you have information about her family? I feel in my spirit, that I should ask this girl for our son, what do you say?"

Alwarappan responded, "Yes you might have seen her. Last time when you came to church you saw her singing in the choir, she also came to our home once. But she is a not a Tamilian. Their culture is way too different from ours."

Amsaveni responded with a convincing explanation, saying that it was not the culture or the language that was important. It was about finding a girl for our son who has those "noble characters of a wife", as mentioned in that

Book, and hoped to get her family's acceptance to marry our son. She expressed the same words of the Book as follows,

"A wife of noble character who can find?
She is worth far more than rubies.
Her husband has full confidence in
her and lacks nothing of value.
She brings him good, not harm all the days of her life.
She gets up while it is still night; she provides food
for her family and portions for her female servants.
She sets about her work vigorously; her
arms are strong for her tasks.
She opens her arms to the poor and
extends her hands to the needy.
Her husband is respected at the city gate, where
he takes his seat among the elders of the land.
She is clothed with strength and dignity;
she can laugh at the days to come.
She speaks with wisdom, and faithful
instruction is on her tongue.
She watches over the affairs of her household
and does not eat the bread of idleness.
Her children arise and call her blessed; her
husband also, and he praises her.
Many women do noble things, but you surpass them all.
Charm is deceptive, and beauty is fleeting; but a
woman who fears the CREATOR is to be praised".

Amsaveni further told that though we may not able to find the perfect partner, still with dedicated prayer and as said in that Book,

"We will commit our ways unto the Creator, and trusting Him and He will bring it to pass according to His will. He who has bought us this far will lead us until the end."

So they decided to ask the pastor about this proposal and contacted him immediately. The pastor listened to them and after speaking to Roshini's family, told Amsaveni and Alwarappan to their surprise, that Roshni's family was equally interested in this marriage. That same day, Amsaveni called up her son and told him that she had found a partner for him, and told him to pray and let her know his decision. The son took three more days to wait and pray for his partner and confirmed his willingness to this marriage.

The wedding date was fixed and both the families were taking turns to visit each other's homes and continued talks. Just in the matter of a few weeks' time, miscommunication crept in due to the language barrier and cultural differences. Slowly it was increasing day by day, and at one point, the marriage was called off. Amsaveni thought she made a mistake. She felt bad within, that due to her decision her son's life had come to a standstill. Amsaveni updated her son with all that had happened and waited for his response.

Her son told her, that whatever happened so far in their lives was never without any trial and testing. He comforted her saying, "He that called us and guided every step of our lives until this point from nothing, will definitely bring joy and peace in this marriage, and in the right time." He also told her to keep everything on hold, all the arrangements and any further progress on this topic until his return in few months' time.

Once he came back, he listened to both the families' unpleasant experiences and had an opportunity to speak to Roshni to discuss their future life. As both her son and Roshni had good understanding between each other right from the initial talks until now, Roshni expressed her concern and assured that she would stand with him on any decision he may take. They both prayed together the same day, for a clear understanding and heavenly favor on this relationship.

Things started working again, but it took almost ten months for both of them to work on the bitterness both the families were going through. As they were both determined to start their married life on their hard earned money and not to depend on their parents or on any loans, they utilized this time to save the money needed and shared the complete marriage expenses between each other. Along with Roshni's sister they planned the whole wedding. With the prayers and blessings of both the families and as a witness to the limitless love from above on both their lives, they got married on 21 November 2010 in Bangalore, in a grand manner.

The marriage witnessed two different cultures, languages and communities coming together in great joy, love, peace and with one accord.

Alwarappan's mother, and all the brothers and sisters of Amsaveni and Alwarappan with their families had come together in one accord for the second time after 25 long years. Both the families met and greeted each other, and had witnessed great joy and peace in the reunion of the family. Everyone's hearts were filled with joy as they genuinely conveyed their feelings on the great favor and grace from above on Amsaveni and her son's life.

Amsaveni's family at the wedding

Amsaveni remembered the words from the Book.

"Eye has not seen, nor ear heard, neither have entered into the heart of man, the things which the loving heavenly father has prepared for them that love him"

All the relatives, friends, and well-wishers who had seen Amsaveni from the time of her hospital return until that moment had witnessed miracles in completion through her life. They appreciated her faith, endurance and perseverance in bringing up her son from her bed-ridden condition, yet keeping the family intact.

Each one of them who witnessed the marriage in their own words acknowledged that,

"With man this is impossible, but with the one who had created heaven and earth, who had guarded protected and provided life to Amsaveni all these years, because of Him all things were made possible."

Alwarappan's family at the wedding

Amsaveni loved her daughter-in-law a lot. She used to tell her about her life stories and how she learnt certain things the hard way. She also told all the essential things of her son's life. She celebrated the differences between their families. She tried to learn "English" in order to communicate with her. On the other hand, her beloved daughter-in-law took the step to learn "Tamil" and broke the language barrier with her in-laws. Amsaveni gave her cooking tips and was very proud of her.

Both the families had shared a great level of love and concern for each other. Roshni's mother used to prepare food for Amsaveni and Alwarappan, and send it to their home frequently. Roshni's sister and her family were a great support and was instrumental in both the families' happiness. After working, Roshni would spend her evening time with Amsaveni, and they both developed a great emotional bond for each other.

After a few months, when Amsaveni's son had sent the visa, Roshni went to Abu Dhabi to be with her husband. After a year and a half on 13th May 2012, they were blessed with a baby girl. Amsaveni was overcome with joy at the news.

All her prayers and blessings all through the nine months of her daughter-in-law's pregnancy was coming to pass in front of her eyes. Yes, she was a grandmother now. She quickly remembered a few lines from that Book which she used to read every day,

"You shall see thy children's children"

"Behold, children are a heritage from above, the fruit of the womb a reward. Like arrows in the hand of a warrior are the children of one's youth"

"Your children will be like olive shoots around your table"

She was filled with joy and her mouth was uttering continuous praise. She called all her brother and sisters and shared the joy and celebrated the birth of their granddaughter with all neighbors around. She called her son and daughter-in-law over the phone again and blessed them immensely with words of life. Here again, she was reading some lines from that Book for both of them.

"Every good gift and every perfect gift is from above, coming down from the Father of lights with whom there is no variation or shadow due to change"

After a month from the delivery, Roshni came to India with her daughter. For the next four months, Amsaveni and Alwarappan had spent every day with the new blessing of the family. Both the families had cherished every moment with the little one. Amsaveni's heart was filled with overwhelming joy, even more than the joy when she had become a mother.

Both Alwarappan and Amsaveni had become child-like when they spent time with their little granddaughter, and both of them spoke words of life and hope to her, and showered her with blessings.

CHAPTER 10

A COMMITMENT TO ETERNITY

Amsaveni lived a life of commitment to all the words she read in the Book. She loved that Book so much, that she would keep reading it as much as possible every day. Though her life was restrained to the four walls and the bed for almost twenty seven years, her spirit was very active. Step by step she was gaining ground, little by little she was conquering all the impossible situations and she left a legacy behind.

She believed that one of the important decisions she took in her life after her hospital days, was her obedience to an eternal covenant as mentioned in that Book. That one line from the Book had really given her the inner courage to submit her and her husband's life, and later her little boy's life for this eternal commitment,

"Whoever believes and is baptized will be saved, but whoever does not believe will be condemned"

From the time she started reading the Book, she slowly started reflecting on herself and her life. Also the clarity provided by the four women (Sheila, Hannah, Suriya and Ruby) in understanding the words from that Book from time to time was very helpful.

In the year 1990, she took this decision. After four years of hospital life and at an appropriate time, she felt she needed to make a choice in order to believe the words of the Book for the rest of her life amidst any situation. Her husband, who by then had a unique experience from the words of the Book, also committed his life a few years (in year 1992) after her commitment. By February 26, 2000 her little boy who had found a meaning in his life had also taken the same decision to obey the commandments of that Book.

All the three loved and respected the words of the Book. As they loved Him, they kept His commandments also. They were cautious of what was said in that Book,

"Unless one is born of water and the Spirit,
he cannot enter the kingdom of heaven"

The choice of that eternal commitment came with a big price of losing the relationship of their loved ones, and it was not an easy choice to disown your previous beliefs and take on a new one. But the words of the Book spoke to each of them in their own life. At an appropriate time, the words of the Book gave a true sense of connection between the creation and the Creator. The heart of the Creator was mentioned in the Book.

The history of creation, the very reason why mankind was created was mentioned in the Book. The reason for all trials in this world was mentioned in the Book. The redemption plan and the limitless love of the Creator towards his precious creation (us) was mentioned in that Book. Every step towards a new life, a new beginning, an eternal hope was mentioned in that Book. The past, present and future of the earth we live in was mentioned in the Book. What Amsaveni read was real, it gave life, it gave hope, and it gave meaning to all her situations. All the tough phases of her life were faced so boldly with the confidence and clarity she rendered from the Book.

It not only helped her but also her husband and son too. She understood that having faith and hope in the true words and obeying them by her actions was an external expression of her belief in that Book. Her life proved **that if an egg is broken by an outside force, life ends. But if the egg is broken by an inside force, then life begins.** For her and her family, many outside forces like money, society, situations, people, status and other factors resulted in a broken life. It seemed there was no way out in each of their lives. But the words of the Book spoke to them in a unique way, in a unique experience all three of them had encountered the Truth personally.

That Truth set them free, it gave them the inside force. The egg was broken by that inside force and for each of them, a new life began. A life so victorious and blessed!!! They not only overcame the situations, they steadily conquered all the outside factors which had given them broken life once. They excelled as more than conquerors.

When did Alwarappan returned to Amsaveni?

CHAPTER 11

ALWARAPPAN RETURNS HOME

Alwarappan who ran away from the situation following his wife's attempted suicide had roamed without hope to all the corners of Tamil Nadu. His own parents ignored him, his brothers and sister did not want to be identified with him, his wife didn't want to live with him anymore. Within the storms of life, he couldn't find a solution. His short temper and laziness had taken his job away from him. He didn't even have any friends to comfort him, as he never had one before. He was wandering without hope and without a purpose. He went from one place to another, slept in the bus stand, washed his clothes in the river, got food from the temples and tried to find jobs for a living.

Days, months and years went by; none of the family members knew where he went, his wife who was fighting for her life in the hospital didn't know whether he was dead or alive.

After her return from the hospital, Amsaveni began staying at her brother's home with her little boy. One day during her secret prayer time, she called her son and told him, "We are going to pray for an important thing today." After everyone had slept her and her son closed their eyes and Amsaveni with all reverence prayed, "I do not know what to speak, I do not know how all my problems will find solutions, and I may be too insignificant to comprehend the Creator's ways. I am constrained to this bed for the rest of my life, my son is very small and I do not know how to provide him education, shelter, values and equip him to face this world, I do not know what to speak, I do not know how all my problems will find solutions, and I may be too insignificant to comprehend the Creator's ways.

I do not know the whereabouts of my husband. But as I keep reading the Book, the words of affirmation, the words of hope and the words of life encouraged me and strengthened me, hence I want to ask these three things to happen in my life.

Firstly, as I believe in all the words of the Book, I would like to ask this in faith; that if my husband is alive let him come and meet us from wherever he is without us going in search of him. Secondly, as a normal mother, I cannot do anything for my little boy but I pray that You will help him, provide him and guide him so that he'll come up in his life learning to face the challenges of this world; and finally as its medically impossible for me to get my senses back, I pray that as how You had healed many sick people, heal me too that I'll get my senses back to live and face this world even in this impossible physical condition."

In just a few months' time from the date of the above prayer from Amsaveni, one day when Amsaveni and her little boy were at home, somebody knocked the door. The little boy went to open the door and saw a man standing there. He asked him what he wanted. The man outside the door mentioned Amsaveni and told that he came to meet her. The little boy ran to Amsaveni and told her that a man standing outside wanted to meet her. She asked him to bring him in.

Amsaveni was shocked to see the man. She couldn't speak. She was awestruck. Amsaveni couldn't control her tears and she wept bitterly. Looking at Amsaveni, the man started weeping. Both of them didn't talk but just cried bitterly for around fifteen to twenty minutes. The little boy who stood puzzled thought to himself that this man made my mother cry. He asked his mother, "Who is this man? Why are you crying?"

In a sobbing tone, Amsaveni replied, "This is your father.

Yes, this is your father for whom we had prayed that night. This is your father who ran away from home. This is your father who was brought back to us by the words of the Book."

Yes, that strange man who was introduced to that little boy was Alwarappan. He told Amsaveni all that he went through from the time he left home until that moment. So much of pain and sorrow he had carried within himself. In all the situations he thought:

"Where then is my hope? Who can see any hope for me?"

He said that one day when he was walking on the road pavement with a depressed heart and hopelessness, he saw a sign on the road with a statement like this,

"So do not fear, for I am with you; I will
strengthen you and help you; I will uphold
you with my righteous right hand."

Just a glance at this word brought a great encouragement to his weary soul. He took that sign and kept it with him. Later, when he started searching for any book in which these words had been written, to his surprise he came to know these words were written exactly in that one Book, which Amsaveni was referring to all these days. That Book which contains the words of life and hope had spoken to Alwarappan in such a unique way and encouraged him to this day. After so many ups and downs, he finally started understanding the truth in the Book.

Both Amsaveni and Alwarappan had again started living as a family with a renewed mind and with a renewed hope. Though his character had not changed significantly, neither his temper nor laziness, yet with all the forgiveness and continuous prayer from his wife, he gradually became a changed man and committed his entire life to the truth he read in that Book. He always wished to spread the good news which happened in his life, his wife's and his son's lives to all the people around him as much as possible. As and when opportunity arise, he utilized it to spread it, as he believed it will be a true motivation and a great encouragement to those men like him. Even until this day, he spends all his time helping and ministering to the people in and around the city of Salem, Chennai and Bangalore by telling them the good things that have happened in his life from an utter brokenness and hopelessness. He renders a great joy and complete satisfaction in doing this as a service to his Creator.

Amsaveni and Alwarappan

CHAPTER 12

IT ALL BEGAN HERE

It all started here. None could comprehend that it was just the beginning of a brand new chapter in her life. It was the path of a unique experience, the life of absolute endurance and perseverance, a life full of hope and confidence, a life filled with joy and happiness, a life that endured all obstacles, a life that could inspire and motivate all who saw and heard about her, a life filled with purpose and meaning.

This was the life that money couldn't give, had no bound, limitless in itself, the one unique experience that's excelled in her life time, the impact which transformed her completely broken and hopeless life in to a glorious beginning.

The way to destruction, continuous failures and struggles, was changed into the way of life, of truth and of hope. Death was beaten once again, she overcame the deadly stings of death once again, and she won victoriously over all the clutches of this world's pain and persistent problems. Yes, she lived for 27 more years from the time she attempted to end her life, way back in Feb 1986, when she was just 27.

She lived for another 27 years, endured and proved to me and to this world, that "There is Nothing Impossible with HIM", the Maker and the Master. It was not the end, it was only the beginning. Now she has resigned from her earthly accomplishments and resides in heavenly peace, a better place to be, an eternal rest, gazing into the presence of the

One who is Omniscient, Omnipotent and Omnipresent, and the only source of limitless love.

She lived for another 27 years, endured and proved to me and to this world, that "There is Nothing Impossible with HIM", the Maker and the Master.

Yes, this is what happened. When the doctors who treated her said that her condition was hopeless and she had no option other than mercy killing, the medical attendant who couldn't tolerate the pain this young girl was going through had suggested to throw her in the ocean and get rid of her. When the whole family was in despair and depression of the continuous stress and helplessness, when the whole world said it is impossible, when all the human efforts failed, she experienced the one unique pre-ordained encounter with that one Person mentioned in that Book, who is the Author and Finisher of our faith.

That day, a lady volunteer (from the Gideon International) who didn't know who Amsaveni was, or where she was from, came into the hospital room where Amsaveni was lying down.

She told her that she would like to pray for her for few minutes, while leaving, she left that Book and told her to read it when she had time so that she will know peace. She didn't insist or compel her. She didn't explain anything about the Book neither did Amsaveni ask what was in that Book.

Later that night, she was struggling in pain because of her bed sores, and her mother who was sitting next to her utterly helpless, just gazed at the unbearable situation of her own daughter. Amsaveni asked her mother to pick up the Book and read it to her without any expectation but just to pass the time.

At that moment, neither she nor her mother realized it would be the game changer of her remaining life.

Her mother picked that Book and started reading it aloud to her. The words read from that Book had started fulfilling its purpose. As it was said in that Book, "My Word that had gone out of my mouth, will not return to me, unless it fulfills its purpose". Yes, as Amsaveni's mother was reading that Book aloud on her daughter's request, something amazing, unbelievable and incomprehensible happened.

Amsaveni started sleeping. It was a miracle!!! Yes, she started dozing off and sleeping. She slept peacefully for eight long hours that night, a sleep which she was longed to have for more than two years, the sleep which all her doctors were trying with sleeping pills and all possible medicines, the sleep amidst the burning bedsores, the sleep amidst groaning pain on the bed for two years, the sleep which would definitely help the external medicines to help her physical body, but actually gave her inner peace. This sleep had not paused all her unending tribulations, but had actually put a full stop to all of it, and had ordained a brand new start.

After that night's sleep when she woke up, she felt a great relief. The pain had not subsided, neither were the bedsores healed, neither did all her physical pain came to a standstill.

But her body started responding to the medicines slowly.

Slowly she started rebuilding her health with the help rendered in the hospital, and with the tremendous support from her sisters, brother and parents, she soon went through a spinal operation where she could now sleep straight facing the ceiling. As the days went by, she recovered very little, but gained new confidence.

She was not ready to face the world right away, but could leave the hospital after the operation. She returned home in the same bed ridden condition but with comparatively improved health, steadily recovering her senses until her hip, and lived the rest of her life boldly and loudly just from her bed.

Her life had proclaimed the words of the Book even in all the twenty seven years of her bed ridden life,

"Great is thy faithfulness, all that I have needed thy hand hath provided, great is thy faithfulness unto me"

Amsaveni started sleeping. It was a miracle!!! Yes, she started dozing off and sleeping.

It was just that one Book that changed and challenged Amsaveni's complete life. History was rewritten in her life, from the day she started believing the words of that Book, the Book which had the eternal word. The word that was in the beginning, the word that was with the Creator and the word was the Creator.

He is the One, who sits in heaven and calls every star by its name, and places his foot on the earth as His footstool. He is the One who left all the glory and honor, and came down to this earth just for the mankind as He had loved the pride of his creation, the humans.

He came in the form of a man, through a virgin birth, lived like you and me, was tempted and tested with all human troubles and trials and was yet without sin, without any spot or blemish. He went up to the cross as an eternal sacrifice for all of mankind born so far and those yet to be born and took all their sins and shortcomings on Him, and had shed the last drop of his blood for mankind's redemption and thus renewed the relationship between the Creator and the creation.

In Him, there is no condemnation, he convicts and corrects but never condemns. He was never judgmental or critical to anyone who came to Him, but always expressed unconditional love as He is the eternal Father. To Him there is no comparison.

He makes a way where there is no way. He delivers His children with a strong and outstretched arm. In Him, rivers of living water flow, and the peace He gives is not like the peace of this world.

As it is said,

"If we confess our sins, He is faithful and just to forgive all our sins, and to cleanse us from all unrighteousness"

By accepting that one Savior who is the one Truth, Hope and Life, her life with all her weaknesses, He changed it all from the beginning to the end.

This Book had transformed the whole generation of Amsaveni, Alwarappan and the little boy from INSIDE OUT, and gave a fresh new start, a brand new beginning, the Book which Amsaveni referred to during the second part of her life, the one source of all her strength and confidence.

The one Book from which she received her first miracle of getting a peaceful sleep, every word spoken in that Book was like honey to her soul. She dearly loved that Book. All her inspirations and peace are from that Book. She had said that when she started believing this Book, the pain did not vanish from her body, the bank balance did not rise instantly, she didn't have solutions for all the problems, neither did she know that she could live through all these twenty seven years in a bed ridden condition. Being completely on bed, without standing and walking but yet, she stood in many people's hearts and had walked triumphantly over all the impossible situations with her sheer faith and determination. It was only possible by the belief she had in the words of that Book.

The source of all her wisdom and knowledge of the Creator and all creation was from that Book, the Book which has the true explanation of how and when heaven and earth was created and why it was created, and how the humans in their weaknesses could meet their CREATOR? It also contains their relationship with their Abba Father, and their life stories and mistakes is what helped Amsaveni to administer her life, endure and pursue her divine purpose.

She adores that Book where the Creator had revealed His heart, mind and His unconditional love towards His creation.

The book which in her opinion has the manual for this earthly life. She calls this dearest Book of hers, as the book that has all the **B**asic **I**nformation (& **I**nstructions) **B**efore **L**eaving this **E**arth - **THE BIBLE**

What's next?

You are not here in this earth by an accident. You are born for a purpose, with a purpose, and to a purpose by Him who created you. You are fearfully and wonderfully made by the very hands of the Creator. You were chosen even before the foundations of this world and even before you were formed in your mother's womb. There is no second person like you ever born in this world or will be born in the days to come. You are Unique. You are created by Him and for Him. For by Him, all things were created: things in heaven and on earth, visible and invisible, whether thrones or powers or rulers or authorities. He is before all things, and in Him all things hold together.

He is the same yesterday, today and forever until the end of this world and the one to come. Let this day, this moment remind you about your Creator and I pray that you will soon discover the secret of your existence in this earth.

I invite each one of you to read that one Book which changed and transformed Amsaveni's life from INSIDE OUT.

By doing so, you will come to know of the One who loved you and gave his life for you, and in accepting Him as your Saviour, you will be with Him forever. The Saviour of Amsaveni, Alwarappan and the little boy will be your Saviour as well.

All glory, honor and praise be to the One who is the Maker and Finisher of our faith.

I dedicate this book once again to the late Amsaveni, my two little daughters and to each one of my readers.

Yours sincerely,

Author
(Edwin Paul Franklin alias Nagarajan).

The author will also be releasing soon an English music album about a friend who can be trusted forever. Watch the space @limitlesslove316.com

ANNEX 1

TESTIMONIALS FROM REAL TIME

1. SHEILA DANIEL
2. HANNAH BENJAMIN
3. ANGELENE SURIYA BENJAMIN

Testimonial about 'Amsaveni' from Sheila Daniel:

We come across many persons in our life but only a few leave a lasting impression on us. One among the few is Mrs. Amsaveni. She was bed ridden because of a suicide attempt due to a family problem. Although in bed, she was always bright and cheerful. Whenever I visited her or talked over phone, her opening words will be, "Praise the Lord, Sister! How are you? Hope you are all doing well. I never forget to pray for you." Her faith in God was unshakable. She accepted Christ as her personal Savior by reading the word of God. God directly spoke to her and He taught her the secrets of Christian life. She thanked God for making her suicide attempt a failure. Always she used to say, "If I had died on that day, I would have gone without knowing Christ." But as Christ is always with her, she has accepted the agony in bed not as pain but as blessing. That is the secret of her cheerfulness. Although living with her parents, brother and sisters who were all non-Christian idol worshippers, she wished to bring up her son as a true Christian. Her praying time was early morning three o' clock. She has told me that God daily woke her up at 3 a.m. and reminded her to pray. She has felt the Holy Spirit guiding her and teaching her the meaning of the verses in the Bible. She had an urge to teach the Scripture to her five year old son. She taught him to pray and read the Bible. She made him memorize the verses. The son, too was obedient and did as his mother instructed him.

Her little boy was very enthusiastic and clever, I encouraged him to learn more verses. He memorized Psalm.119:1-176, the longest chapter in the Bible in just three months, when he was only seven years old. He recited the psalm in the School assembly and got the first prize in

Memory Verse Competition. He attended Sunday class in a church and there too he won many prizes. The seed sown in his heart took root and he became a true child of Christ. He was baptized at his teen age.

Her son is a model to the present day youth. He was a loving and caring son. He took good care of his mother. Many days he used to cook, clean the room, wash the clothes and nurse his mother. He respected the elders and paid heed to their advice. His faith in God and his prayer life is rewarded. God has today placed him in a very good position. He sought the Lord and the Lord lifted him up.

Almighty Father listened to the prayers of both mother and son and one fine day, Mr. Alwarappan became a true son of Christ. God gave him the patience to look after his wife. He too wished to serve the Lord and his only aim was to do His ministry. Father, mother and son lived separately in a house and dedicated their life to Lord Jesus Christ.

Due to Mrs. Amsaveni's prayers and the prayers of her well-wishers, her son is at present working as a Regional Representative for an International Embassy. God has lifted him up before the eyes of his relatives. "If you honor Me, I will honor you" says the Lord.

Her son's marriage took place in Bangalore in a very grand manner. I was very glad to attend his marriage. That was really a great witness to his friends and relatives. Even in his marriage he honored his mother by making her sit in the front row in her wheel chair. She prayed and blessed the couple in front of the gathering. Her daughter in law too is a true child of Christ and God has blessed them with two cute little girls.

I am really thrilled to watch Mrs. Amsaveni's endurance amidst all atrocities. May this work transform myriads of people and may everyone who read this book come at least one step closer to Christ. May our Almighty Lord shower his blessings on all the readers.

SHEILA DANIEL,
ASSOCIATE PROFESSSOR OF ENGLISH,
GOVT.ARTS COLLEGE FOR WOMEN,
SALEM.

Testimonial about 'Amsaveni' from Hannah Benjamin:

It is a great privilege and honor for me to write my relationship with Mrs. Amsaveni. I came across so many people in my life but I could boldly witness that Mrs. Amsaveni's family is precious and remarkable. She was successful as a life partner, as a mother and as a woman of faith in action. I'm sure the God above is very happy and delighted in her.

As I could remember the first instance I met her was in her home, through Mrs. Krishnaveni her younger sister who worked with us in our school. Amsaveni was a forsaken woman and felt loneliness in her heart though she was in amidst of her parents and relatives. The Almighty God brought some friends into her life and I'm privileged to be one of them. We use to visit her as much as possible and helped her understand the precious book of all times (THE BIBLE) and when she accepted Christ she never felt loneliness until her death. She depended on HIM for everything. She became a woman of prayer and strong in HIS words and HE had met all her needs miraculously every day. Her faith and confidence in God is a great encouragement and model to us. She became a great testimony to all her family members.

She was a successful Life Partner to her husband. She prayed for her husband and through her life he was lead to the truth of the Word of God. Because of her continuous prayer and commitment he became a servant of God and doing HIS ministry until now. I used to share her testimony to encourage many women to stand firm in God. Among all the difficulties and sickness, she was very faithful to the words of the Bible till the end of her life.

She was a successful mother. She taught her son how to pray and enabled him to study and memorize the word of God. She encouraged him to follow the Creator, work hard and study well. Because of her love and prayer, her son Edwin Paul Franklin is living as a child of God. She passed on her faith and godliness to her son. Edwin I believe certainly will pass on this legacy to his children and this blessing will follow from generation to generation.

I want to quote what she said one day when I called her, 'Hannah, One orange is enough for my dinner and I thank God for giving me this today'. I felt, this is a fine example on how she lived her faith in action. She left a great legacy of faith to this world and to us who read her life.

HANNAH BENJAMIN,
PG TEACHER IN ENGLISH,
GOVT. HIGHER SECONDARY SCHOOL,
YERCAUD, SALEM.

Testimonial from Angelene Suriya Benjamin, India:

As I look back the 24 years of my union with Mrs. Amsaveni it is one of the things for which I am most grateful is the rich and varied fellowship which I enjoyed all over the world because of her faith, testimony and who shared joy in the Gospel and her desire to make known the unsearchable riches of Christ.

And she is the representatives of the hundreds of other women I knew and loved over the years. I guess we're all able to point to new and life-enhancing experiences during the years following our commitment to Christ. Our new riches are many and varied, and we probably enjoy and appreciate them to a greater or lesser extent, depending on our needs. For me, one of the greatest discoveries was the remarkable galaxy of Mrs. Amsaveni women of God who seemed to radiate Christian leaders and not only being able to identify with what they said but also to sense an almost tangible personal and family bond.

Mrs. Amsaveni conveyed to this young author and hungry Christians the essential ingredient of the new nature – a Christlikeness which was appealing. How appropriate then that this book 27 +27 on Mrs. Amsaveni is linked so closely with Christ. For surely it's our Christlikeness which is at the heart – which is the heart – of our witness. As you read this book on Mrs. Amsaveni "Let the beauty of Jesus be seen in her".

It is my hope that others may enjoy these varied glimpses of this book and that the Lord whom she loved and served may be glorified. A book like this owes much too many. I warmly commend this book.

ANGELENE SURIYA BENJAMIN,
HEAD OF INSTITUTIONS,
ANDERSON SCHOOLS - INDIA.